I'M YOU

I'M YOUR MOTHER

Christiane Collange

Translated by Helen McPhail
Edited by Gillian Willy

ARROW BOOKS

Arrow Books Limited
62–65 Chandos Place, London WC2N 4NW

An imprint of Century Hutchinson Limited

London Melbourne Sydney Auckland
Johannesburg and agencies throughout
the world

First published in France as *Moi, Ta Mère* by Fayard 1985
First published in Great Britain 1987

Printed and bound in Great Britain by
Anchor Brendon Limited, Tiptree, Essex

ISBN 0 09 948220 7

‘It is parents who love their children
not children who love their parents.’
Françoise Dolto

ACKNOWLEDGEMENTS

My thanks first of all to my four sons, who for thirty years have made me ask myself so many questions.

Next, my thanks to Mac, who never left my side during the writing of this book. His intelligence, his application, his adaptability, his co-operation, his steadiness, his swiftness have transformed my work as a writer.

Mac is a friendly nickname: his real name is MacIntosh.

CONTENTS

FOREWORD

IF your daughter smiles as she says good morning,
IF your son kisses you as he says goodnight,

IF your daughter enjoys what she is studying,
IF your son studies what interests him,

IF your daughter tidies her room once a week,
IF your son polishes his shoes once a week,

IF your daughter brings you an aspirin when your head aches,
IF your son asks how you are when you look worried,

IF your daughter sets about organising her summer holidays in the spring,
IF your son starts looking for a summer job at Easter,

IF your daughter sends her grandmother a card when she's on holiday,
IF your son brings you a little present for your birthday,

IF your daughter plans her finances and sticks to the plan,
IF your son lets you know when he won't be in for supper,

IF your daughter turns out the light when she leaves the room,
IF your son locks the front door when he goes out,

IF you consider your daughter more mature than you were at her age,
IF you consider your son happier in himself than you were at his age,

. . . you don't need to read this book, except to confirm that you are perfect parents.
Since not all fathers and mothers are as wise or as lucky as you, think of them – lend it!

I

Pity The Parents

I'm suffering from 'child-ache' – rather like having toothache, or a headache.

It's a dull, general sort of pain, not bad enough to keep me in bed or away from work – not even enough to keep my mind off other things, or make me lose my sense of humour. Yet all the time there's this cloud hanging over the horizon of the new day. It gradually sours our relationships, damages our feelings for one another, spoils each day because it won't go away. And, as time seems to slip by faster and faster, each day is so precious to me.

As I've had enough of this malady, I've decided to put down in writing how frustrated I am – I don't feel I can stand feeling like this any more. It breaks my heart that I can't seem to get my feelings of loving tenderness across to you.

And I'm not only emotionally upset – my whole being seems to cry out. I've always been such a strong believer in the virtue of communication, the value of a liberal education, the importance of trust and being allowed to grow up in freedom without the crippling effects of restriction. I've always tried to be understanding, to find out why there have been disagreements, and where I've gone wrong. I've wanted to appreciate what you needed from me and what I expected from you, and to adapt basic rules to prevailing circumstances. I must find out how these factors have changed our feelings for one another so that we have ended up in this sorry state.

No more smiles or kisses

When my children were small I felt guilty because I never seemed able to give them enough. They were always so demanding, and I gave them a lot of loving care, but they were never satisfied. Sometimes I felt overwhelmed by their endless need for affection, though on the whole I was fulfilled by it. A child's smile or hug always seemed a more than adequate return on my investment of motherly love.

Now that my children are older, nothing seems to be right. They are still very demanding, but they don't want my love and attention any more. Our payments system has broken down. They have no more smiles or hugs to spend on me, even though I've lowered my prices – very often two words would be payment enough.

'Good morning' when they come into the room I'm sitting in.

'Thank you' when I hand them the car keys.

'Good night' when they get down from the table as they gulp down the last mouthful.

'Please' when they borrow my pink jacket or go off with the magazine I've just bought.

(Not to mention a reasonably interested 'How are you?' on days when I'm off colour.)

If only they could occasionally understand that at times I'm prone to moods of weariness, melancholy or weakness, just like anyone else – in fact, just like them. But that doesn't mean that I'm not still brimming over with love for them which is there for the taking provided they treat me as an equal and not as a person who's not quite all there.

Perhaps this state of affairs is partly my fault: I've never really suffered from depression, and I'm generally in a good mood when I get up in the morning. I've always been a 'capable woman' rather than a 'poor old Mum'. Considering me pretty tough, they've never really had to learn to handle me with care.

However, whether I'm weak or strong, I'm not

prepared to put up with this new relationship, if it can be called such a thing!

It's just possible that my revolt has something to do with my instincts as a modern woman. I've never felt a call to martyrdom or sainthood. I have always campaigned for the freedom of the downtrodden and for the right of every man and woman to choose his or her own way of life. As a feminist almost since I can remember, I am proud of the place which women have carved out for themselves in society, as well as of the new relationships we have managed to establish between many men and women.

This new deal between men and women didn't just come about. We had to exchange opinions, question preconceived ideas, re-think relationships – a sprinkling of tenderness and a pinch of laughter were the finishing touches for this new recipe for loving – they helped to make it lighter and more appetising.

Because of taking part in what I consider to be an unquestionable step forward – the emancipation of women, whose second-rate role in society had not been of their own choosing but had been forced on them by ancient tradition – I have become convinced that it's better to tackle problems head on than to let them slowly gnaw away at your life.

So I'm going to be daring, and admit something I shouldn't. Without a doubt I love my children, but this feeling of love is not enough to fill me with joy and satisfaction. **As a mother I'm frustrated and I'm not proud of it.**

There are two sides to the generation gap

I'm fed up with hearing young people everywhere saying how terrible it is for them being on bad terms with their parents. It happens the other way round too: there are parents who feel rejected by their young, that they can no longer communicate with them. No one ever talks about *them*.

There are two sides to the generation gap – it is equally difficult to cross from either side. I often think that my arms aren't long enough to reach out to the young people on the other side, to help them have the courage to reconcile their inconsistencies. At other times I think completely the opposite; they just don't want to take the plunge and become responsible grown-ups – they're much better off on their side of the gap, and nothing in the world would make them want to cross over to our busy kind of life with all its problems.

To make sure we don't try to drag them out of their cushy hide-out over on the other side of the gap, they pull up the gangplank, batten down the hatches and shut down the radio.

We can't imagine how to get on board with them again, or even re-establish radio contact.

One evening last winter I was watching on television the umpteenth report on pre-delinquent adolescents – or post-adolescent delinquents, I'm really not sure which. In the closing shot a sly-looking young boy sighed heavily and said, 'I do so wish I could have talked about all this with my parents, but in my family we don't talk to each other . . .' The final close-up was heavy with significance about these bad parents who, by refusing to talk, forced their child to confide in undesirable people, only too ready to lead him off the straight and narrow path.

As a matter of fact, there are very often times when I would like to talk to my children about important matters. But in our house, even though we don't live in a drab council estate, we rarely speak to each other about anything other than everyday matters. 'Can you let me have some money?' 'I haven't got any socks left.' 'Why did you get Pepsi again? You know I like Coke better.' 'Hasn't Victoria phoned me?' . . . But I'm not worried about trying to improve our sparse communications. I have learnt from books to say 'I', not 'You', and to say exactly what I think instead of stepping gingerly round the issue: 'I can't stand you playing your music so loudly when I'm working' rather than 'How do you manage to work with your music so loud?' I can't be accused of not speaking my mind. But they're the ones who don't want to listen to me, and refuse to discuss anything. They really don't care what I think or how I feel.

Pity the parents of today's youth! We are accused of their misdeeds, it's our fault when they go wrong, the media produce any amount of psychiatrists who point the finger at us – we are the excuse or alibi for all their wrong-doing.

Well, I don't agree. I don't think we've been such bad parents. It hasn't been easy to bring up children in a changing society – a consumer society when all the traditional values have been thrown overboard, and every-thing can be bought or thrown away at will.

I would love to know how our parents would have coped – they were always telling us how they managed so much better than we did. But we haven't had a war, so our children haven't had to learn how to go without or be afraid. We haven't had a Victory to make heroes of us all and give us the chance of rebuilding the country for our children.

Children who've been pampered and spoilt

I know that it's not the thing to do to question our relationships with our children; if we don't get on it's bound to be our fault, all the experts tell us so. The teachers are only too ready to rap us over the knuckles when their pupils – who, incidentally, happen to be our children – give them a hard time because they just couldn't care less.

After all, we only get what we deserve; if our children are badly behaved it's because we have spoiled them.

There's nothing we can do, we can only accept that we're stuck with the roles we have given ourselves of liberal parents – and liberated mothers. Whatever the cost.

With our greying hair and granny glasses we must above all be generous and pay up even if we don't stand a chance of getting anything in return.

It doesn't enter your heads, you children, that we would dare to criticise your behaviour. You say:

> Well, Mum and Dad, you can't grumble . . . You wanted us, didn't you, and you had us. We didn't ask to be born. You can't have it both ways and expect us to be grateful as well. Careful, Mum, if you say you're not happy because we don't give you enough, and demand too much from you, you'll risk being called inconsistent. The Pill had already been invented when you had us. If you weren't prepared to accept us as we are you shouldn't have had us: all the shrinks will tell you that.

Possessive mothers, over-effusive, Jewish mommas, fussy, tearful, Latin mamas are out! The understanding and ever sympathetic Mum is in!

The dream mother: independent, not too possessive, who doesn't smother youthful ambitions, doesn't upset one's ego, above all doesn't interfere with the next generation . . .

What nonsense! I haven't got any complexes – Oedipus really doesn't influence my behaviour. I've never fancied going to bed with any of my four sons. I have been successful enough in my professional life not to need reflected fame or glory through my children. I have so far escaped the hot flushes and depressions associated with the menopause. I promise you I have absolutely no wish to keep you with me for the rest of your life. I'm quite self sufficient and a lot more liberated than most of your girl friends who make a song and dance about their independence but won't accept responsibility.

Actually, I am convinced that I need you less than you need me.

It's your dependence which is a burden to me, not my own!

The argument that time passes

You must realise that I'm talking to **YOU** personally now, not 'you children' as I did when you were small. It was always 'Bathtime, children', 'Teatime, children', 'I would tidy up your things if I were you, children, or there'll be trouble' or 'I'll get you children some chocolate eclairs if you leave us in peace on Sunday morning'.

Now you're nearly grown up and 'you children' doesn't apply any more. It's one or other of you, each in your own way that you upset me, worry me, make me absolutely furious or wildly happy.

All this amazes you. You really can't understand what's come over me all of a sudden, and you think it's definitely not on to discuss our disagreements in public. OK, maybe everything isn't perfect between you and the wrinklies, but there's no need to make such a thing of it.

The answer is I've just got to put up with your hurting me until one day you take it into your head to stop, but in the meantime I'll go on supporting you. It'll all end up all right when you have children of your own which you will want to park on me when you need to get rid of them for a bit.

Perhaps that's cynical, and there's no proof of it yet . . .

You must understand that I can't convince myself any longer that we're just going through a bad patch and that in a few years we'll have forgotten all about it. The argument that everything gets better as time passes has helped me to put up with you at thirteen, to bear with you at fifteen, to accept you at eighteen, to tolerate you at nineteen. Now you're over twenty, and I can't go on pretending – I don't believe any longer that, having weathered the storms of your adolescence and your interminable post-adolescence, we can automatically re-establish our relationship which broke up so suddenly nearly ten years ago.

It's because I believe that what is happening between us is quite a pity, rather sad and could become irreparable, that I hope to get to the root of the problem and find out what it is that's poisoning our relationship, by objective (and, I confess it, subjective) analysis. I need to sort out my inner confusion a little and show you what makes me tick – how I react, why I laugh or cry, how I live . . .

Just this once, and I promise not to make a habit of it, we're not going to talk about you, but about me.

Why me? Because:

I'm your mother . . .

II

A Character Who Doesn't Exist

I'm not a young mum or an aged mother; no one acknowledges my existence – just someone who has given birth to human beings who, having been infants, toddlers, children and then adolescents, are hanging on to their youth like grim death to put off becoming grown up.

There is proof that I don't exist: I am ignored by opinion polls. In December 1983 when this book was already beginning to take shape in my mind, I seized on an enquiry in a news magazine. The title couldn't have been more apt as far as my current thinking was concerned: '**WHAT SORT OF PARENTS ARE YOU**?'

The introduction intrigued me:

> To be a parent: this is without doubt the greatest and most delicate responsibility that anyone can take on. It is a skill which has changed more radically than any other . . . Shaken up by a constantly developing world, forced to keep up to date with their children, to make their own rules as they go along, how do parents react? Are they happy or unhappy, confident or unsure of themselves, strict or liberal? In attempting to portray these parents we have employed a laborious but revealing method: the opinion poll. To work it out carefully with the Gallup Poll experts, we first questioned all those who are in touch with parents: psychologists, sociologists, teachers.

Just imagine my excitement! Although I'm always a bit suspicious of self-righteous, not to say hypocritical, 'psychological/ sociological-educationists', I hoped I was finally going to find some objective answers to my subjective questions. To be able to compare my own experience and that of some dozens of other parents whom I had consulted with the opinions of thousands of my fellow-parents, and the verdict of a representative sample was exactly what I had been looking for.

Total disillusionment set in, however, a few lines further on, when the pollsters described their approach more fully:

> We decided not to give a breakdown according to social status or level of intelligence, but to look at three 'ages' of parents: those with very young children, those with schoolchildren of 6 to 11, and those who are bringing up adolescents.

The age of the adolescents was given a little further on in the enquiry: from twelve to sixteen years old.

And so what about me? Where do I come in? Isn't anyone going to ask my opinion? My problems, my responsibilities, my educational theories, all my thinking – aren't they really of any interest?

After all, I'm supporting children of more than sixteen years old, I fully share with them the agonies of choosing a career after (or instead of) A-levels, I'm just as scared about unemployment as they are, I pay for all their comforts – and costs rise every year – I put up with their ups and downs, stand by helplessly as I watch them suffering the agonies of love, I am liable to be blackmailed, whether deliberately or not, threatened by delinquency, drugs or even suicide. Aren't I allowed to say something as a parent?

Just because the age of majority has been reduced to eighteen am I considered a retired mother? Written off, past it? In other words, just pay up and shut up!

Do people really think that once our little darlings reach their majority they immediately take charge of their lives and relieve us of the cost of educating them? Just because it's practically impossible to make any constructive suggestions to them without getting the brush-off does that mean we should give up trying?

To tell the truth, I was rather shocked but not absolutely amazed. I've got used to the way the media hide away everything that isn't wildly exaggerated into a sort of black hole of Calcutta. You have to be exceptionally handsome, excessively rich, unbelievably poor, miserably unhappy, terribly young or older than God to hit the headlines or be of any interest to opinion polls.

At my stage of motherhood, I'm not really anything in particular – not particularly young or old, not ecstatically happy or desperately unhappy either. After all, you've all grown up strong and healthy. That should be enough to make me happy in my motherhood. I've done my duty and produced you and you've got everything that's needed to go out into the world.

Then why do I feel on edge? It must be because things have changed.

Toffler describes this situation well in *Future Shock* and *Third Wave*:

> All the difficulties of adaptation experienced by modern men and women stem from having to face up to unprecedented circumstances, with no established pattern, no previous reference, no way of conforming to the behaviour of earlier generations.

That explains the stress I'm under as a mother – we and our children are experiencing something completely new: post-adolescence.

All life's stages are postponed

In the old days – and I won't call them 'the good old days' because I think for a woman it's much more exciting and certainly more comfortable to be living in this modern age than three or four hundred years ago without running water – imagine heaving buckets of water all day! In the old days the lives of mothers and children interwove much more closely, rather like a relay race. When the mothers were young, the children were small; when the children grew up, the mothers were old. One handed on to the other and continuity was assured: when the parents were no longer strong enough to work, the children took over. Maybe they didn't have much fun but the rules of behaviour were pretty easy to understand.

If you didn't feel like supporting your parents in their old age, you disappeared. You could choose between being a deep-sea fisherman or a priest, a servant girl or a nun – you had to find some way of earning your living as the price of your freedom – you could choose between working for other people, or for God.

As people aged more quickly and young people grew up sooner, their lives slotted into each other pretty neatly.

If by chance some mothers failed to age quickly enough to fit into the system, they had the decency to disguise themselves. Black dress, black shawl, black stockings, you could see exactly what they were.

As time goes on, the situation becomes more complicated and the characters involved less straightforward. For the last hundred years the two vital stages of our lives that overlap have got wider and wider apart:

1. The moment when you decide to make your own way in life and become an adult, relieving us of our responsibilities;
2. The moment when we're beginning to get past it, and it's your turn to look after us.

The legal school-leaving age is later, and further education takes longer (you need at least five years to get any sort of diploma that will ensure you a job) – there are fewer shotgun marriages . . . Being young has been prolonged way beyond childhood.

Physical preservation, better health, improved quality of life have all postponed old age.

Therefore you have had nearly ten carefree years before you have to face up to financial responsibility – from fourteen, the old school-leaving age, to twenty-four, the age when, with a bit of luck, you get to the end of your studies; that is, of course, if you haven't had to do too many re-takes. Then there's the delay while you look for your first job: you can usually count on several months between applying for jobs and actually finding one you like.

Speaking for ourselves, we can expect to live an extra twenty years, and we're not just leading longer lives, the quality is higher too. Improved diet, preventative medicine and taking part in sport have dramatically improved the last part of our lives.

This means that more often than not we find ourselves all together under the same roof for ten years, in roughly similar situations: mature people in the prime of life.

An investigation by the national institute of demographic studies in 1982 showed that of young people between 18 and 25 half were living with their parents. The others had had to leave home – either because their studies or their employment meant they had to live elsewhere – or to get married (31%) – or to live with someone (10%). Therefore, excluding the statistics for young marrieds – but, in this case, do they still count as 'young people'? – the results of this investigation are even more surprising: three-quarters of young unmarried people between 18 and 24 still live at home.

According to Catherine Gokalp, who directed the investigation, only six per cent of young people decided to leave home because they didn't get on with their parents. That doesn't include the growing number whose marriage or relationship broke up, which brought them back into the family fold once they were on their own again – on their own, or with a child. On a temporary basis, of course, but for how long?

The problem is that moving back home when you are no longer a child creates deep misunderstandings. We still think of you as children, try as we may to see you as adults like us.

You still expect Mummy and Daddy, or maybe Providence, to provide everything for you without taking into account the fact that the time for independence – or sharing – has arrived.

In fact, the boot is now on the other foot. It's no longer a case of us holding on to your hand – it's you who won't let go of our apron strings.

The Irish Method

In my day – I have to use this expression which annoyed me so much when I was young, with its rather revolting aura of nostalgic moralising – young people, exasperated by the frustrations of having to live with interfering and domineering parents, would walk out so they could live as they wanted to. The less rebellious ones got married, which was a more gentle way of doing the same thing. Until that day when the children left, the parents always had the final word about what when on in the household. 'If you're not happy you can get out!' the father would roar as the mother sat there silently, fighting back the tears. The threat was usually enough to quieten the rebel, with its implication of being cut off with a shilling, never to return; except, possibly, as the Prodigal Son, all repentant and full of remorse – or, better still, as the rich cousin who had made his fortune abroad.

In any event, the position was clearly understood: you achieved your independence by the sweat of your brow.

That didn't stop the occasional little hand-outs, marriage settlement, bit of help in the right direction, or legacy; but since good bank balances make good families, he who held the purse-strings also imposed his principles and way of life on the household, even down to meal times.

Nowadays, things have completely changed; instead of leaving home when they feel they would rather like a bit of independence, the young have adopted the Irish method: they hang on to the comforts and benefits they have already got, at the same time demanding their independence, resorting to terrorism if necessary.

Their weapons are drugs, delinquency and suicide. The illegitimate baby has to some extent been withdrawn from their terrorist arsenal by the availability of legal abortion, but most parents quite rightly still hate the idea of this and much prefer contraception. Abortion blackmail is therefore still partially effective.

Not all young people use these dangerous weapons; but because of a few heavily publicised examples, most parents are willing to pay up, since they would do anything rather than be guilty of not helping any of their children when in danger.

The worst kind of blackmail

Where girls are concerned, suicide is the most popular weapon – a bottle of sleeping pills, a dash by ambulance to hospital in the middle of the night, stomach pump, two hours of agony trying to understand, overcome with self-reproach and self-accusation, ready to forgive all. An outburst of weeping next day, and the distraught parent will do anything rather than have to re-live those unbearable moments.

How do you avoid giving in to this sort of blackmail? You can't imagine anything worse than the death of your own child, let alone its suicide, when the horror of death is added to the torture of guilt. How can you help feeling responsible for this act of desperation, for having failed to hear, or indeed to listen to a cry for help?

Luckily, girls almost always fail. Their instinct for self-preservation helps them realise very young, as soon as they reach secondary school, that when it comes to barbiturate poisoning, it is always a good idea to leave the bottle by the bedside so that the duty doctor will immediately know what to do. There is another traditional precaution, which is to leave a note on the kitchen table saying that you are going to commit suicide, and where; or to ring up a friend and warn her, so that you can be rescued as soon as possible.

I have heard this same story from the parents of no less than ten girls. Luckily the drama ended safely in rescue ten times, but how well I understand the mother and father who give in to their daughter's every whim thereafter, even if they are positive that she did not really want to die. All their weakness is excused by the nightmare thought of a second attempt.

Do these girls who play around with their lives realise what they do to their parents? It's all very well to talk of the thoughtlessness of youth, but surely there are limits. Please, please you girls, don't brandish this weapon of fake suicide just to find out what effect it will have on your parents. If you really think deeply, I believe your strong female instinct for survival will tell you not to die in your prime, and that there are much better things to do in life, such as having a baby. So spare us. You wouldn't consider it human to drown a kitten in front of its mother, so how can you inflict the same sort of torture on your parents?

With boys, suicide is generally much more dangerous. When young men play with death they usually mean it. They use more effective weapons, such as guns or ropes, and succeed more often. Also, they rarely use suicide as a threat to get what they want from their parents. Their terrorist arsenal is different, and no less deadly: violence, running away, delinquency and drugs – especially drugs.

Today you smoke pot: yesterday you were on the booze

Taking drugs is like committing suicide by degrees, a slow and pernicious way to destroy one's life. Parents react in exactly the same way as described above: the same terror, the same guilt.

We've been told often enough that boys who take drugs are victims of their family circumstances, unloved, deprived of tenderness. This must certainly be true in some cases, but not all.

What parent today can feel safe from this plague? In the smallest country town, in the most conservative areas, joints are handed round in the playgrounds. Very often it's not lack of parental love, but young people's need to conform that makes them pass the dope around to see what sort of a 'high' it produces. Our parents did not feel any guilt for the drunks of our generation, so why should we be responsible if our children take dope?

It's not always our fault.

I have written that in bold type mainly for my own benefit. I really need this kind of self-forgiveness to restore my poor maternal ego, so undermined by my guilty conscience.

I'm so envious of those proud parents who can boast that their daughter is going to marry an eminently suitable young man, or that their son has just got into one of the best universities. 'Just like his father and grandfather before him – all the eldest boys in our family passed out top!' I envy them the glory reflected from their child; it must be wonderfully comforting to believe that natural justice exists for good parents.

Good parents have good children. Bad parents have bad children. There are still some parents who agree with this reassuring equation. When I meet them I am envious of them, just as one is envious of:

. . . couples who celebrate their silver or golden wedding and still hold hands lovingly;

. . . employees who get on fantastically well with their boss and feel thoroughly appreciated in their professional field;

. . . holidaymakers who tan without getting burnt;

. . . people who love food and can eat lots of cake and chocolate mousse without putting on an ounce;

. . . women who admit calmly that no one can always stay the same;

. . . men who remain faithful through love and not because they are afraid of being caught out.

I am envious of those successful parents, but I can't share their simple faith in parental justice. Otherwise, how can you explain the number of fine men whose sons are drop-outs, or real brutes whose children have joined Band-Aid?

The direct link between upbringing and excellence was taken for granted by our predecessors. And as a certain percentage of people still turn into successful adults in spite of everything, their parents can grow old peacefully, justified in their own eyes, and those of society, by the accomplishments of their children.

For our generation of parents, clear conscience has been ruled out. Thanks a lot, Freud! Parental responsibility, particularly maternal responsibility, is only ever exercised in one way: wrongly. If things go badly, it's bound to be the parents' fault. If by any chance childhood does not end in total failure or profound inadequacy, then that's entirely to the child's credit. He is obviously a strong character who has managed to throw off his complexes and come to terms with himself in spite of a difficult childhood.

Childhood is always difficult: that is the basis of psychoanalytical theory. If it is passed in a happy and affectionate atmosphere, the challenge lies in escaping to establish one's own personality which is being smothered by an excess of affection. If, on the other hand, the child has been subjected to family quarrels, whether actively or passively, he or she has to get over these conflicts in order to fulfil his or her repressed and severely damaged emotions.

I really don't want to be held forever responsible for everything that happens to you and all your generation, but I can't rely on either public opinion or psychiatrists to let me off the hook.

So you see that, at your age, the only person who can really release me from you, is you. If you agree to do this, we could start again and build up a different relationship, one where you wouldn't need to scare me into doing what you want. A relationship which would be more like democracy than guerilla warfare.

Therefore, for your benefit I'm going to outline my plan of action – I'm going to try and explain what my policy has been, describe any outside circumstances which have influenced what I have done, and do my best to put into some sort of order the philosophy that has governed all the years that I have devoted to motherhood.

III

First Of All, I Do Love You

Let's get things straight: if I am so concerned about all this, it's only because I love you. Otherwise it would be much easier for me just to drop all our disagreements.

On days of head-on confrontations, scenes or let-downs, evenings when you've made me so miserable I cried, nights when I have lain awake for hours worrying about you, I honestly have asked myself: Do I really still love you?

Yes, even though it may shock you, there have been times when I have questioned my feelings for my own children.

Can this traditional mother's love, so overpoweringly strong towards tiny, helpless little creatures, begin to fade or even disappear altogether when the fluffy little chick becomes an ugly duckling? Can it really be transformed into aggression, rivalry, disregard or rejection when frustration and disappointment become altogether too overwhelming?

In the case of mammals, it is obvious that the mother's link with the new-born is essential for its survival. Once the young are able to look after themselves, the mother can dispense with this link which is no longer needed. As nature arranges these things so well, the females are able to forget last year's family and concentrate all their energies and attention on the next one.

When you give away your pet's kittens or puppies, mother and babies do not see each other again. If they meet some months or years later there does not appear to be the slightest recognition. They behave like animals of the same breed, but not at all like members of the same family. This fact is even more striking where the fathers are concerned, as they show no recognition of their own offspring (except for male birds, which show greater responsibility, perhaps because the male is more involved in incubation than in gestation).

It is not therefore unnatural that our mother-love should gradually fade, at least where female animals are concerned. The strange emotional tie, distinct from sexual or reproductive instinct or the need for preservation, which mankind calls love, is not an automatic consequence of being a mother. Bearing young ones is not enough in itself to make a mother look after them all her life. There must be a subtle chemistry which helps them to understand all that concerns their young. This is what we call feelings, and has nothing to do with the deeply instinctive bonding of a female to her new-born young.

In due course, should not these feelings diminish or even disappear as the young one grows from infancy towards adulthood?

My generation has recognised that love is a perishable commodity, and that the laws of our society cannot force us to go on living with someone whom we no longer love, until death do us part. Divorce by mutual agreement is now legal, an established and accepted part of our culture. If one can cease to love a once adored partner, the father of one's children, friends who were once very close, even brothers and sisters when disagreements become the norm, then surely one can equally well cease to love one's children?

Quite honestly, I don't think so.

Before rushing to disagree, and quoting dozens of examples of heartless mothers or, more exactly, joyless mothers, let me explain.

Cold-hearted mothers

It appears there are some women who feel neither tenderness nor a sense of responsibility towards their children. They have children as a result of social pressures, not because they really want them. If they have an opportunity of getting rid of their children by handing them over to a nanny or a grandmother, sending them to boarding school or letting their father have custody if there is a divorce, they take it. They are popularly referred to as 'more feminine than maternal' in preference to calling them what they really are: 'bad mothers'.

My own feeling is that one should pity them rather than condemn them. It is never easy to put up with your children, large or small, even when you find them irresistible, but a mother's life must be absolutely unbearable when there are no loving feelings to make up for sulks and tantrums. Much of what is known as housewife's depression seems to me to have more to do with being a mother than with being a woman. Might not impossible children really be unloved children?

How else explain the fact that the noisiness and irritating habits of other people's children seem so annoying? And vice-versa! One always says, when a grizzling or tyrannical five or six-year-old is making his parents' life a misery, 'How on earth can they put up with a child like that?' Because they love the child, that's why. Without that love the child's ghastly behaviour would be just too much for them.

Having made a study of cold-hearted mothers I have come to the conclusion that they show all the symptoms of a lack of love rather than a failure of love. Most of them didn't just stop loving their child one day, they probably never loved him in the first place.

In spite of all the reliable principles we've learned about motherhood, it is possible not to love one's child. The child may not have been wanted, the parent may have wanted a girl instead of a boy (usually it's the other way round); maybe it's because he looks like his father whom you no longer love, because he gets in the way of your freedom or your career, or because he's too ugly or stupid . . . we had better stop there!

Quite honestly, I believe that when a mother does not love her child, she very soon realises it and so does the child, even if nothing on earth would make her admit such unnatural feelings. It seems that only on the psychiatrist's couch could people bring themselves to make such a horrifying confession. We all know the disastrous effect such unnatural feelings have on us psychologically; they are the excuse for all our neuroses, the pretext for all our rebellious feelings.

Sadly, not much can be done to avoid this unfortunate situation: love can't be made to order. Neither for an adult nor for a child.

Women's DUTY

To make up for this lack of feeling which could end up with a child being abandoned, or even murdered, Western society has invented the notion of DUTY.

DUTY was my grandmother's favourite word. Everything in women's lives which was difficult, boring, unpleasant, tiring, frustrating or repetitive, was their DUTY. It was supposed to make inconstant women faithful, extravagant women thrifty, anti-social women friendly and, above all, to transform into respectable mothers those women who, deep down, really couldn't bear their own children.

DUTY condoned women who were strict and beat their children to relieve their own frustrations. Let those who have never punished, slapped or smacked a child under the pretence that it was for his own good dare to contradict!

Another advantage of the DUTY theory was that it encouraged some mothers to give vent to their destructive instincts. As long as they fulfilled their DUTY by providing for their children's physical well-being and their intellectual training, they could with a clear conscience cross them, suppress their creativity, impose on them a way of life or a religion which they might hate, suppress their sexuality, neglect their most basic need for tenderness and disregard their innermost feelings.

That was indeed a good time for bad parents, even if the children were hardly ecstatic!

For good mothers too things were simpler. Thanks to

the Holy Virgin, whose veneration was at its peak in Catholic countries, devoted mothers wore halos. All their excesses of affection were forgiven, their generosity was admired, their self sacrifice was prized. Even though they sincerely adored their babies and motherhood gave them genuine pleasure, they were regarded as absolute saints, models of virtue and devotion. They weren't considered idle if they didn't earn their living, if they had three months' holiday in the country during the summer or if they foisted themselves on their children well before retirement age because they'd failed to make provision for their old age.

Being a good mother meant doing just what you liked with a clear conscience!

The very expression 'a good mother' is rather misleading. It introduces a moral dimension, as if loving children could be 'good' or 'bad', or love were an item in a moral code. And yet to love one's children is more of a bonus, like being attractive or clever. Just as it's possible to make the most of one's appearance, keep one's figure, develop cultural interests or exploit artistic gifts, it should also be possible to influence and improve family relationships. Under one condition: you must be able to melt at the sight of a little thing that is as unattractive as a larva!

You don't fall in love just because you want to, and you don't love a child just because you have brought it into the world, or adopted it. There needs to be a magic cocktail of anticipation and tenderness, eagerness and appetite for life. But once a mother has given her heart to a child, that love hardly ever fades with the passing of time, which is not always the case when a man and woman love each other.

It doesn't fade, but it changes. Just as well really, because if I tried to take you in my arms now, when you're miserable after failing an exam, or you've had your wallet stolen, or you've twisted your ankle playing tennis, we'd look a right pair.

Motherly love changes, but it doesn't disappear.

How else do you explain that, whether or not you tell us about them in so many words, we feel for you so acutely in all your ups and downs? When you fall in love we are in suspense as much as you, waiting for the phone to ring, desperate in case the latest conquest lets you down – we know how you're longing to see her on Saturday. When you're ill we worry desperately and imagine the worst even when it's only a cold or a hang-over. When you feel low we get depressed – when you're cheerful we feel happy.

If that isn't love, then what is it?

Three fundamental changes

One could even argue that modern mothers love their children better than their grandmothers did. I can see my grandmother turning over in her grave at this remark – how could I, a modern working woman, who is divorced and sexually liberated, love my children more than she did.

I didn't say **more**, I said **better**!

The upheavals of the second half of the twentieth century did not create only difficulties in our family lives. Three radical changes have affected our status as mothers – and fathers – and have strengthened our reasons for loving you:

1. **Contraception and legal abortion.** These two revolutionary trump cards have ensured our complete physiological freedom, enabling us to have only the children that we really wanted. Since wanting and loving go well together, the more we wanted you the more, obviously, we loved you from the moment you were born. Of course I am not saying that all those babies of former times who 'came a bit too soon' or 'were little afterthoughts' weren't welcome, but still, there is a very special emotional bonus for the baby who arrives according to plan.
2. **The reduced birthrate and smaller families.** Demographic and economic experts may be in despair over today's standard one- or two-child family, but it

increases the importance of each individual child. Scarcity is always highly valued, and children are becoming scarce.

3. **Better standards of living for most people.** We have never had to go short of food in order to keep you fed, nor go without holidays to provide for you properly. The consumer society which was a great help to us when you were tiny has meant we have been able to bring you up without sacrificing too much. We shared with you the benefits of an expanding economy, and it is a good deal easier to be loving and generous when there is no shortage of basic essentials.

In fact, not only did you not interfere with our lives, we always considered you an integral part of our pleasures in life. Families are smaller nowadays, but childless couples are also rarer. Never before have so many women sought help so that they can have a child. Artificial insemination, test-tube babies, adoption of Third World babies, anything is better than being childless.

Adult conversations are devoted to you

Do we have to admit, at the risk of encouraging you to take advantage of your position, that, as far as we are concerned, you are unique? It is unbelievable how much of our adult conversations are devoted to you, and this becomes more so with the passing years.

When you were little, it was enough to be asked how you were getting on, and replies were short. After all, one's fellow-conversationalist would hardly be enthralled by how well you had taken your bottle, or how you had enjoyed your first day at nursery school. Such achievements are only interesting to grandmothers or paediatricians – they bore office colleagues to death, and kill family gatherings – not to mention what they do to men, who find that sort of conversation deadly.

As time goes by, your successes, and particularly your setbacks, are of great interest to other parents. They rhapsodise enviously over your achievements, and identify fearfully with your disasters.

A proud father tells a roomful of strangers that his daughter has just got into medical school. A mother, hitherto unable to make her presence felt, is listened to in respectful silence while she describes how her son has refused to go on holiday because he has to work hard to pass his finals.

On the other hand, everyone starts talking at once if you ask for advice on what sort of school or crammer would take a child who has just been chucked out of school. The reason they all join in is because they have all gone through a similar experience. If you don't look out, this boring subject can easily monopolise the conversation for the whole evening, without even getting on to the general subject of independent schools, or the reform of university education. You could say sometimes that forty- and fifty-year-olds spend more time discussing their young than such classical topics as politics or religion. Heaven knows why!

Sometimes when I'm with my friends – I have real friends too, like the ones you have at your age, whom I can discuss almost everything with, who share in my giggly moods and come to my rescue without demanding an explanation, who have adolescent or post-adolescent children like me – we can all grumble together and really let go our feelings, which we can't do in front of you. We can comfort each other as we discover whether we really have got the worst kind of problem children at home or whether we can count ourselves lucky – we may find others are infinitely worse off than we are.

During these sessions we come out with the worst horror stories we know just to frighten ourselves. In that way we manage to console ourselves by comparing our own trials and tribulations with those of other parents.

A classic device of the popular press.

It is like the story of the poor princess, dripping with diamonds and lying in her palace, just having had her fifth miscarriage. She is crying between her satin sheets because her lord and master, the prince whom she adores, wants an heir. Poor princess, will she be discarded? Reading about the poor sterile princess and feeling quite overwhelmed by the burden of the domestic chores awaiting her on her return from the office, the unfortunate working woman with her two children who still need bathing, feeding, comforting and scolding, feels greatly bucked up: she can forget the piles of washing and the bills for a few moments and thank heaven for her fertility!

We're like that over drugs. We can always quote the friend of a friend, or perhaps the sister-in-law of one of our directors, who found a syringe in her teenage child's bedroom: just for a moment we don't feel quite so bad about the smell of cannabis we noticed in the flat the last time we went away and left you for the weekend. As long as your 'high' goes up in smoke we don't need to panic. Just get a bit worried.

Just because your older brothers smoked pot a few years ago without getting hooked on hard drugs doesn't mean we don't get scared to death every time we see you teetering on the edge of addiction. 'I dreamt that my daughter injected herself with drugs in front of me,' said one friend, still shattered by this nightmare. 'She stared me straight in the face as she stuck the needle in her arm. I tried to reach out and stop her, but my hand wouldn't move. I wanted to cry out but I couldn't utter a sound. It was ghastly. I woke up absolutely drenched with sweat, I don't think I have been so frightened by a dream in my whole life.'

Maternal love has no rules

It's true, we shudder every time, all of us. Because our relationship with each child is unique. Strange as it may seem, the fact that all is well with one child doesn't solve another one's problems. Each child has his own exclusive place in our hearts and in our preoccupations, whether he makes us happy or sad.

Some children fill you with happiness and others don't, but that doesn't appear to have any connection with how much we love them. It affects only the joy that they give us.

It is often surprising that the least rewarding or least affectionate child in a family will take up the greatest amount of the parents' conversation and concern. The more rude and unkind he is to his parents, the more he seems to be on their minds and the fonder they are of him. His brothers and sisters, more considerate, more studious and well behaved, rebel against this unfairness. They forget that love has no rules.

Maternal love just as much as any other kind.

It may be that attachment to a child derives from the very fact he is unique. It has no equal in other human relationships. In the case of an unhappy marriage one can seek consolation with another partner for a few days, for a few months, sometimes for even longer. Disappointed maternal love cannot find consolation through another child, or by having more children.

I remember a mother of seven children. Her family was delightful, the children lively, outgoing, gifted and friendly. One of her daughters, the third, had died at the age of twelve. Ten years later she confided to me: 'I have never got over it. Every day I think of her, every day I want her back. The gap which she left in my heart has never been filled. The rest of the family are marvellous, I love them deeply, but I miss my special little girl who was different from all the others.'

No friend or lover can ever replace a child in a mother's life. There are many divorced women who forgo the chance of starting a new life because they think their child will not get on with the new man in their life. They are often wrong, and the child would probably have settled down very well in the new household, but they prefer not to take the risk. Consciously or unconsciously, they are convinced that they can get over losing a man, but to sacrifice a child would be unforgivable.

Young people are only too well aware how precious they are to their parents. In the long list of the grievances, lack of love comes last. Year in, year out, when they are asked what they think of us and what they might hold against us, their replies are always surprisingly positive.

It was in 1982, in a Catholic-inspired weekly magazine, that the 13- to 17-year-olds confirmed their good relations with their parents: 96% with their mother, 83% with their father. 'Teenagers and Their Parents, Everybody's Happy!' was the feature's title.

During December 1983 and January 1984, a communist Sunday paper arranged an independent opinion poll of 15- to 24-year-olds. It appears from the wording of the questions that the newspaper was hoping to detect some unease, even unhappiness. Answers about the family proved the reverse: 80% of the young people considered that the family 'is not going out of fashion', 81% that 'you can rely on your family when you have problems', 75% that 'home is the best place to be'. Not much of a revolution going on there!

In May 1984 a TV magazine commissioned a poll of the 10 to 15 age group. 79 per cent of them considered that their parents got on well together, implying that they were happy with their family atmosphere and that they tended to idealise their mothers and fathers. When they were asked where they gained the greatest benefit or learnt most, they put their parents in fourth place, after school, friends and reading, but ahead of television and their local neighbourhood.

So everybody's happy?

As far as the young people are concerned, it would appear YES. The overwhelming majority really have no complaints about us. They have got us pretty well trained to tolerate their particular ways and habits. Occasionally they have to threaten or shout to get what they want, but that has been their well-tried weapon since infancy, and it still proves itself very effective. In fact they find us quite easy to live with, even pretty reasonable.

The heavily publicised image of rebellious young drop-outs, left to their own devices and the dangers of the streets by neglectful mothers and resigned fathers, may well be partially accurate, but it is scarcely representative.

Parents, on the other hand, are by no means so enthusiastic.

OUR list of complaints is long. Minor disagreements over practical details, major clashes over important decisions. WE don't agree. WE are not happy.

IV

Minor Details Produce Major Rows

When you were little, you shouted and yelled, demanded and protested – you dirtied your nappy again as soon as I had changed it, you woke us up in the middle of the night and stopped us from having a lie-in in the morning. You made me plan fourteen meals a week and you invaded our privacy – in fact, you turned our young married life upside down.

And yet we put up with this harassment in a fairly relaxed way. As parents we forgave you: children know not what they do.

Wasn't it our job to bring you up so that you would gradually learn to conform to the elementary rules of society? We realised we would need a lot of patience to accomplish such a superhuman task; to transform into a civilised and disciplined individual this lovable but unruly little creature that for some strange reason we had decided to bring into the world.

The trouble is that even after years of hard work trying to teach you that you must show consideration for others even though it might seem against your own interests, you still charge into our daily routine like bulls in a china shop. As to everyday good manners, yours seem to get worse every year.

From when you were born until you were ten or twelve we were generally able to register progress apart from some particularly hard cases. Little by little, by drumming into you the same 'What do you say?', 'Thank you who?', 'Say hello when you come in, say goodbye when you go out', 'Rinse out your toothbrush when you have finished using it', 'Leave your school books tidy if you want to find them tomorrow morning when you go off to school', 'Don't put your muddy shoes on the sitting-room chairs', there was some undoubted improvement.

Not that there was always order and harmony – far from it. Still, when you went off to spend the afternoon or a few days' holiday with uncles or aunts, or at a friend's house, we would sometimes receive compliments: 'He/she was delightful, so well behaved!' These comments always surprised us. It did not seem to us that we shared our household with a sweet little girl or a splendid little fellow. But we were pleased; our advice had not gone unheeded. At least you knew how to behave with other people.

Things began to go wrong at the very beginning of adolescence, when secondary school studies began in earnest. Using the earlier morning start and increased homework in the evenings as your excuse, you let your good habits slide. Disciplinary habits as well as good manners.

Hundreds of parents can confirm my experience. What happened in our house was no worse than in anyone else's.

When there are adolescents in the house, the place is a shambles!

When you got to twelve or fourteen, your bedroom began to look like a junk shop, then a stable, and now it can only be described as a rubbish dump. (Since puberty usually begins earlier for girls, the chaos in their bedrooms begins a year or two sooner.) I know – all I need do is shut the door and turn a blind eye to what's going on in there. That is actually what I decided to do fairly soon – to go into your pit as little as possible. I conceded that it was your territory, and if you were happy to live in such a pigsty I didn't want to have anything to do with it. Anyway, the closed door suited us both: it spared my wrath and protected your sanctuary.

I only venture in for a great clear-out once or twice a year, when you go off on holiday with your friends. The Augean stables do have to be cleaned out once in a while if you don't want us to be invaded by rats! On these occasions I only throw away what's obviously rubbish:

empty sweet papers, piles of cigarette ends in one of my best ashtrays which I've been hunting desperately for months, empty record sleeves, old newspapers, comic books with nearly all the pages missing, dead batteries, odd socks, bald tennis balls, empty beer cans, etc.

In spite of meticulous care not to throw away anything vital, I always get into trouble when you get back for throwing away THE scrap of paper which was your only record of some boy or girl's phone number, now apparently lost to posterity.

I apologise. I manage to look penitent, although I'm quietly determined to do the same thing the very next time you go away, mainly because of the smell of stale tobacco which threatens to pervade the whole house. Anyhow, I think you only make a fuss on principle. I don't think you're all that much against having your room tidied up for you occasionally. If you didn't complain you would have to say thank you, and that would make you sick.

So we would be able to achieve a modus vivendi if only you'd stay in your lair. But you won't, you overflow your boundaries and pollute our environment. **You don't respect MY territory.**

You don't understand, and seem surprised that I should say such things. You don't want to invade my territory, you want to stay clear of the house as much as possible – you don't want to get involved in our dreary middle-class existence.

How to maintain my surroundings

I have to tell you: your state of chaos gets on my nerves – a hell of a lot, every day, almost every hour of the day.

Do you want to know why? Well, I'll tell you. In the morning, when it would be nice to find the kitchen spick and span at breakfast time, I find myself having to pick up all kinds of bags, wrappings, boxes and empty bottles left lying around from the night before. There's nothing more horrible than a messy kitchen when you've only just woken up!

In the evening, dirty glasses and breadcrumbs litter the table when I am trying to gather up strength to get the supper ready after a day's work at the office. On Sundays you vanish without warning, having emptied the fridge while we were out getting some fresh air. In the holidays you'll eat anything, at any hour, and never stop to consider that a plate can be put away tidily in the dishwasher in as little time as it takes to leave it in the sink. And so I put away, I throw away, I wipe down, I continually tidy up the mess you have left.

I can't get used to your casualness. I really don't think I'm paranoid about being tidy. Quite the reverse, like all working women, I've always got through household chores with an eye to speed rather than perfection. I don't have a thing about hoovering or polishing the bathroom mirror. I just want to keep things neat enough not to offend my aesthetic sense. I don't do housework for the sake of it, I do it for my own comfort.

That's why it irritates me so much when you mess up everything that I've taken the trouble to leave reasonably straight.

All parents are in the same boat. Your offhandedness defeats us. We find it very difficult to understand your monumental contempt for everyday matters.

Why? For heaven's sake why?

Why can't you ever turn out the light or shut the door when you leave a room?

Why can't you ever put back a dictionary or a telephone book when you've used them?

Why do you always make the pencils, biros and notepads disappear which have been carefully placed by the telephone or in the kitchen to write down important messages or shopping lists?

Why do you never replace the roll of paper without giving a thought to the next occupant of the bathroom?

Why do you throw your jackets or coats on to the furniture instead of putting them on a coathanger?

Why do you take OUR sunglasses or OUR bathing

towels without bothering to tell us so that WE only notice they're missing when we want them?

Why do your personal papers and passport get lost regularly, along with anything important that you were supposed to be dealing with? Why do you leave the petrol tank empty on Saturday evening when we want to go out and the service stations are closed?

Why do you forget your candidate number when you sit a public examination, and your examination certificates when you are applying for a university place?

Why do you forget the front door key when you come back at two in the morning so that we have to get up and open the door when we're fast asleep? (I've specially asked for that to be printed in bold type in memory of the hundreds of hours of sleep we've lost thanks to you!)

After all, you can't say we haven't said, stressed, emphasised, repeated time and time again, in every possible tone of voice: 'Don't forget, put it away' . . . '*Put it away, don't forget*' . . . 'DON'T FORGET, PUT IT AWAY' . . . '**PUT IT AWAY, DON'T FORGET**' . . .

And yet we invariably end up getting infuriated and cursing that for the umpteenth time we're having to ask the same person to do the same thing.

When I make this sort of comment you give me a look of supreme irritation and contempt, as if I were a boring little suburban housewife, only interested in the polish on my parquet floor or the perfect symmetry of my sheets in the linen cupboard. Such contempt shocks me because I'm quite convinced I work a thousand times harder than you – that I'm at least as concerned as you are about the world we live in – that I think as deeply about our society and its future as you do, and I have to spend far too much time on small everyday matters.

Of course it's boring tidying up and thinking about possessions, but if you neglect them they get their own back by getting dirty, broken or lost.

As we're not yet living in the robot era when, according to your science-fiction books, these machines will take over everything from us, our manual tasks, our memories, even our brains – I get landed with the things you haven't done. Anything you can't find I have to look for: if it has disappeared, got lost or been stolen I have to replace it.

I'm your mother, not your daily.

I really don't see why I should slog away at tedious little jobs while you lie sprawled on your bed for hours, listening to your music. I'm sick of picking up your things from all over the place, and tired of ironing your shirts because 'You're so good at it, Mum'. I've had enough of taking back the empties to the bottle bank, and of missing the beginning of the TV film because I had to finish tidying up the kitchen. I love idling about too.

Incompatible hours

And since we're going in for a few home truths, let's go the whole hog and discuss your attitude to time. The twenty-four hours of your day no longer correspond in any way to the fourteen hours of activity and ten hours of rest which make up our own days. Although we live under the same roof, we always clash. You're asleep while we're awake, you wake us up when we're asleep; you eat while we're working, you come in just as we're leaving the table, you feel hungry when we have just finished putting all the things away . . .

The only time when we find ourselves at one in our requirements is between six and eight in the evening, when we want to use the phone, only to find that you're on it for hours on end, either because you are ringing up other people or they are queuing up to ring you.

Like your organising ability, your timekeeping has been gradually deteriorating since you reached adolescence. It's impossible to understand how anyone's biological time-clock can alter so much between childhood and adolescence that sleeping and waking become completely reversed. The same child who, for ten years, jumped on our bed on Sunday mornings because he was hungry and wanted to play while we were still half asleep, can't nowadays utter a word when he staggers heavy-eyed from his den at two o'clock on a Sunday afternoon. The little girl who had to be carried to bed because the sandman had already passed by at eight o'clock while she was watching the television in the sitting room is now quite unable to close an eye before two in the morning. That starving brood who happily sat down to eat with their parents at least twice a day – three times on Saturdays and Sundays – has turned into a gang of larder-raiders, their unpredictable cravings for food never apparently coinciding with our own hunger pangs.

These are shattering transformations, and extraordinarily irritating.

Fathers often seem to get more annoyed than mothers over this casual disdain for time. No doubt their memories are more deeply ingrained with recollections of their own fathers sitting down for their dinner at seven thirty on the dot: hours had to be respected.

At that period time was more specifically a concern of men since they had to fit in with the outside world. Women and children therefore had to submit to their timetable. It is only recently that domestic time has become a matter for discussion, open to negotiation to suit everyone's needs.

'What time are we eating tonight?' – a question which would have been inconceivable at the beginning of the century: dinner was always at the same time. A one-way question by the middle of the century: the housewives asked, the husbands decided. An open question for the last quarter of a century: the answer varies according to the different requirements of the household. But unless you take the trouble to ask, you won't get an answer, and it's no good dashing out in a panic in the morning and reappearing at nine in the evening, most indignant because there's nothing to eat.

Once more, you are infuriated by any comment from us on this difference of opinion over timekeeping. Why can't we leave you in peace to live at your own pace, sleep when you want to, eat when you feel like it, study all night and stay in bed all day if that appeals to you?

I examined my conscience dispassionately one day when you accused me of being absolutely obsessed by time;

I discovered two deep-seated reasons which explain my irritation, and why I consider it so essential to sort out this problem of time.

1. *A future reason:* Your refusal to conform to a 'normal' routine makes us anxious for your future. Those of us whose living and working hours coincide with the majority of the population know that we can't claim night and day as our personal possessions. We're not free to appropriate them and rearrange them according to our own wishes. To earn one's living within the society, to fit in with any kind of commercial activity, it's necessary to be able to talk coherently before lunchtime and to sleep at night rather than all morning; it's vital to be aware of the time, and keep appointments, and it's no good pretending to be amazed when you 'find out' it's an hour later than you'd thought. In fact, we're dreading the moment when you have to give up your nocturnal habits and adopt a more normal attitude to day and night, because it seems that the nearer you get to the point of embarking on your working life, the more chaotic your own daily routine becomes. Isn't that absurd?

2. *A present reason:* your contrary timekeeping seriously upsets our life. Occupying the same house as we do, we're always clashing because our daily routines no longer have much in common. Since classic periods of time, such as mealtimes, sleeping time and working time no longer coincide, we either have to put up with you coming and going at inconvenient moments, or protest strongly in order to safeguard our sleeping time and keep to our mealtimes. None of this exactly enhances our moments of relaxation, conversation or rest, and it helps to explain why our bad temper is both chronic and chronological!

I'm grumbling because it is *my* time you're wasting by being so casual. And I would much rather spend my spare time on things I like doing than on these little daily dramas.

Male chauvinist behaviour in the young

Well, of course, it's elementary, my dear Watson. All these irritations and frustrations which are making me feel tense and shrewish, and the reproaches and innuendos are instantly recognisable! It's the housewives' lament – it's exactly what we were proclaiming twenty or thirty years ago when we raised the standard of revolt against our lords and masters, who used to come home and expect to just sit down and be waited on without thinking of lifting a finger in the house. That was in the days when their hours ruled our lives, and they would be astonished if the meal wasn't ready as soon as they felt hungry.

Do we have to start fighting the battle all over again with our children, now that we have achieved victory over their fathers?

The men themselves have certainly changed. Your dear fathers would never dream of behaving as you do. They understood long ago that it's not only the women who work in the house. They realise that they are just as capable as we are of laying a table or clearing it, of cooking supper or shopping in the supermarket. They've learnt that women can feel just as exhausted as men, and that two pairs of hands can do twice as much as one when it comes to housework.

We have taught them this, using gentle teaching methods and practical demonstration, preferring this way to nagging and shouting. You can see the results: you no longer come across undomesticated husbands unless their wives like them that way.

It's you young who behave like male chauvinists now. You assert your rights and power of persuasion, insist on good service, are selfish and insensitive, are uncooperative, etc. etc. . . .

Is there no female equivalent of 'male chauvinist'? Someone ought to invent a word. This method of getting what you want is not restricted to boys alone. Thanks to equality of the sexes and co-education, girls too act the 'madam'. When they're studying just like boys, they take advantage of the situation just like boys. Susan admits it:

'My pharmacology course is really very hard – I just don't have time to cook for myself, do my washing or phone the doctor for an appointment. Mummy is fantastic, she sees to everything. Why should I go and live away from home? I may move out when I've finished my studies, but certainly not till then' . . .

Not all parents are as 'fantastic' or available as Susan's mother. Louis has looked after his two children from the moment his divorce came through and has been a doting father for more than ten years. He considers the way his daughter takes advantage of him absolutely shocking: 'And there was I counting on her to help me bring up her young brother! It's all the other way round. My son of fourteen manages more or less to feed himself, but Madam, using her law degree studies as an excuse, never lifts a finger in the house. So in the evening it's me, after my ten-hour day as a physiotherapist, who's slaving over a hot stove. If I don't cook, she doesn't eat. If I don't do the shopping she stuffs herself with horrible sweets which don't do her health or her figure any good. The result is that I do the shopping and the cooking in a bad temper. And then she complains because I'm not much fun!'

Poor Louis, he would be very surprised if I told him that he was practising feminism unawares. He has found out the hard way why working women one day revolted against their accepted status.

The real male chauvinists still had, in general, one good argument in their own defence: they often worked hard, earned their living, sharing substantially in household expenses when they did not bear them completely. Their wages justified their demands in their own eyes, even if not always in ours.

This obviously does not apply to you. Not only do you not earn anything, not only do we have to keep you clothed and fed, but you have the nasty habit of flinging **our** money about on what **you** want.

This problem of cash, loot, dough, is the bane of our relationship. It would be pleasant not to have to discuss it. And yet, how can we ignore your outstretched hand?

V

'Can You Lend Me A Fiver?'

This woman really upset me. We were in the middle of an office outing. Her anger was so like mine on occasions! The reason why she expressed herself more forcefully was that she was considerably worse off than me financially.

Her twenty-year-old son had recently crashed the family car in a silly accident. Leaving a party one Saturday night, he and his friends decided to have a race down a narrow road. He went too fast, lost control of the car – he's only recently passed his driving test – missed a corner and landed in the ditch. By a miracle, no one was badly hurt, just one sprained wrist and a few bruises. But the car itself was a wreck, the steering bent and all the front smashed in. Beating out the panels and putting everything right would cost more than fifteen hundred pounds – a fortune for a couple who had taken early retirement . . .

And of course, the car was only third-party insured. As no one else was involved, there was no question of being able to claim it back on the insurance. They would have to cut down on their summer holiday and dig into their savings to get the damage repaired.

'The worst of it is, he didn't even dare come and tell us about it. When he saw what he'd done to his father's car, he left it by the roadside and just ran away. The first thing we knew about it was when the police came to tell us the car had been found abandoned. You can imagine how worried we were, we were afraid he'd been hurt. He came home on Monday morning, when I'd gone to look after my elder daughter's children. He shut himself up in his room and he didn't even take the trouble to ring me. It was only that evening, when I came home, that I found him sitting in front of the television as if nothing had happened. I slapped him, not to punish him, of course, but to relieve my own distress. I had been frightened, I was so angry with him.'

The poor woman was still furious. She was genuinely shocked. Not only had her son placed a severe and unexpected financial burden on her, but he had not even apologised or expressed any remorse. He just managed not to make a scene when she announced that in future he would have to wait until he was earning his living and could buy his own car before showing off to his friends.

'I gave in to him too much, I spoilt him. When he was little I never refused him anything. We weren't well off – his father was an electrician and we had three children – but we never went short of anything in the house. And I was always ready to go without things myself for the children's sake. I can't complain about my elder children; they did well at school and have got good jobs now. But I spoilt this one. And now it's too late, he's got into bad ways over money. Just at a time when his father has had to retire early and we have to be even more careful. You'd think he bore us a grudge.'

Of course I sympathised with her, but in a sense I felt comforted: I wasn't the only unfortunate person to have financial entanglements with the younger generation.

The casual generation

Whatever the parents' social background and standard of living, the unholy trinity of parents, children and money produces the same conflicts: on one side are the parents struggling to balance their budget in times of economic difficulty, and on the other their children, spending-mad, used to living in the lap of luxury and completely irresponsible about money.

I must honestly admit that parents are to a large extent responsible for this youthful prodigality. Carried away by their increasing prosperity in the years before the first oil crisis, they forgot to teach their children how to manage their finances. Nothing was too good for them; they had quantities of sweets, and each year brought more and more tempting new fashion fads. Everyone went on holidays abroad, electricity and petrol seemed as natural and free as the air we breathed. No one dreamed of getting shoes mended, finishing a loaf of bread or darning socks. In these conditions, how could children be expected to learn about economising?

You can add to this the old European obsession about not discussing money in front of the children, whether to worry about it or to enjoy it. One can understand why this generation, brought up in the casual atmosphere of the consumer society, can't accept the constraints of the Western economic crisis.

The habit of asking 'Can you lend me a fiver?' several times a month is therefore not restricted to a small world of executives and prosperous middle-class families. Nearly every family has rows over money. Money is always at the centre of the conflict because it is the symbol of independence. Young people can't be genuinely liberated and financially dependent at the same time.

And here we see again, amongst young people, one of the truths thrown up by feminist struggles: financial independence has a profound effect on personal relationships. It is very difficult to proclaim one's freedom when one can't support oneself, even partially.

Sorry, but you can't at the same time ruin us and ignore us, hold out your hand and write us off. There is a direct connection between the umbilical cord and the purse strings.

Four kinds of fraud

You are obsessed by all this money business; we are driven mad by it.

Cash lost, cash stolen, cash wasted, cash lent to friends who never pay it back, cash for essential fees, never-ending cash for dressing up in the latest fashion, cash earned by parents and spent by their young. Some stories you hear are just plain sordid.

Jane, a teacher, had a ring at her door one day. A very respectable lady introduced herself. 'I am Ben's mother, he's a friend of your son Jeremy. My son tells me that he borrowed fifty pounds from your son and hasn't paid it back. I have come round myself with the money. Please could Jeremy not lend Ben any more money. It's very important, because Ben owes money everywhere. His father and I are having to go round his friends to pay them back. I apologise, on his behalf as well as ours. *Please* don't forget to tell Jeremy.'

The wretched mother said all this very quickly, rather red in the face. Jane felt embarrassed at seeing her humiliation. She was worried too: how could her son have lent so much money to a friend? Where had he got it from?

She questioned Jeremy when he came in. The answer, after some moments' hesitation, was devastating: 'I didn't lend him the money. Ben's gone too far, I told him ages ago not to do it.'

'Not to do what?'

'The trick of borrowing money.'

'What trick?'

'It's a way he's found to get money out of his parents when they don't want to cough up. He looks upset and says he's in debt, that he owes thirty, forty or even fifty pounds to one of his schoolfriends. His mother doesn't approve. She wants to pay it back, but since she doesn't trust him she doesn't give him the money, she takes it round herself. Usually she comes across the friend and gives him the money, and asks him, as she did here, not to lend any more to her son. All Ben has to do is to get his mother's money back from his obliging friend, and he gives him twenty per cent commission to keep him quiet.'

Jane went straight round herself to give the five ten-pound notes back to the mother and explain the trick. She was resigned. 'He used to pinch money from my purse. It was better.'

Tricks like sneaking notes out of Mother's handbag or Father's pockets, the rake-off when you run errands for us, the ten pounds advance on the allowance which is never paid back, the over-estimating of school requirements, pick-pockets on the bus, school playground extortion, the friend who is going to reimburse you – you have tried all these tricks. So did we, at your age. Our parents turned a blind eye, as we do, at the same age. Between parents and children a certain amount of fiddling is allowed – when it scratches the surface without seriously upsetting the family budget.

Remembering our own penniless youth – aren't we all hard up when we're young – we took a fairly relaxed attitude towards the way you fiddled your school money accounts, but your insatiable need for money is very often just too much. Not being able to keep up with this constant demand we have begun to say NO, with the result that you have perfected various more or less fraudulent ways of squeezing cash out of us.

1. Hidden expenses

Some bills aren't paid in actual cash. We pay them automatically without being able to control them or make a decision about them beforehand. The telephone, for example. This infernal instrument gobbles up our confidences for hours on end, and then sends us the bill, which is quite indecipherable because, for years past, the phone has refused to divulge the details of our calls – a completely hidden expense which is deducted from our bank account.

It sometimes seems to take you more than twenty years or so to realise that this sort of deduction diminishes our bank balance by exactly the same amount as would a cheque or the equivalent in five pound notes! More than twenty years or so for you to realise that **a bank account has to be provided with funds**!

You have a very basic attitude to the telephone: it's as essential to you as the air you breathe. But as it doesn't cost you anything to use it at home, you can't see any connection between the costs of home and public telephones. You can see your money being devoured in a phone booth. When you ring us up from outside, you speak briefly without wasting time on trivial matters such as your health. If we dare ask a question or try to get a bit of news out of you, you cut us short with, 'OK, 'bye, I haven't got any money left – we're going to be cut off.' At home, on the other hand, you're inexhaustible. Sometimes we've counted up to twelve the number of times you say 'OK, 'bye' before finally hanging up.

I heard a ghastly story of a young American girl who came to spend a month as an 'au pair' with a French family. Every evening when she was baby-sitting she would call Mom and Dad in Chicago. In the States, when you call long distance a telephone operator asks you for the number you're calling before putting you through. Here, no one asked her anything and, since she could dial straight through automatically, she was convinced that the telephone was free. The family received a bill for about £400 at the end of the summer. Almost what they would have had to pay a proper nanny. They didn't dare send the bill on to the States, but each summer since then they have been careful to restrict the use of their telephone to local calls.

In fact, we tend to dread the summer season. Your best friends go off to stay with their grandmothers miles away in the country and, since your generation wouldn't dream of communicating by letter – they take much too much time and effort to write – you spend your life on the telephone.

Even at other times of the year we get bills which turn out to be quite inexplicable, and in November the bills double. Parents first interrogate each other, then imagine that the computer must have gone mad. So they write a letter of complaint to the Telephone Manager, which is almost always denied. Next they suspect each other of carrying on a mysterious relationship with someone miles away in the country, or, possibly, abroad. Finally, of course, they find out that the fascinating new friend you met on the beach last year lives in Birmingham, Edinburgh or Nice.

You get upset, when you move into your own flat, at having to settle your bills every quarter. Usually you fail to pay them, and the telephone or the electricity is cut off. And what is your immediate reaction when faced with such a crisis? To ring up Mum and Dad and tell them how unfair and beastly it is to do such a thing to their poor little girl or boy.

And yet it's not as though we've failed to grumble about how much the telephone costs, or to point out to the family at supper that charges were about to be raised again.

(It should be noted that parents of girls feel more threatened, since they are even worse about the telephone.)

Electricity and other sources of energy share the same phenomenon. Your inability to grasp the principle of cause and effect between a burning light or a radiator left on and the drain on our finances is so well known that I won't go on about it.

Yet there are other, more insidious, costs. Have you, for instance, ever thought about how you're wearing out the car engine when you roar off with screeching tyres, or how you're spoiling our surroundings when you damage the paintwork or wreck the chairs – not to mention the danger to our carpets when you leave glasses lying around on the floor? All this carelessness will have to be paid for one day, and it won't be cheap!

2. Stopping payment

This financial expedient enables some businessmen to avoid bankruptcy. They admit their difficulties and a receiver is appointed whose job it is to pacify the creditors and keep the company going until an honorable solution is arrived at.

You adopt the same principle when you are in a particularly precarious financial state. Discovering that you can no longer satisfy your creditors, you tell us all about your debts and the loans you can't pay back, and ask us to bale you out. On a temporary basis of course. Loans are always temporary when you ask for them, but they tend to become permanent once you have got them.

If your creditors are powerful enough to be a real nuisance – perhaps your bank manager is threatening to sue you unless you immediately replace the amount you have drawn by cashing a dud cheque for the third time – we will rescue you, just to avoid having to watch you leaving the house handcuffed to a policeman.

Unlike you, we are frightened and horrified by the thought of dud cheques. We don't fool around with banks because we've known for ages that they have absolutely no sense of humour and are merciless when someone defrauds them. Of course, they've got money, but they're not in the habit of handing it out to young spendthrifts. Occasionally they show a little humanity, and don't get too angry when things first go wrong, but this good mood never lasts long and they always end up demanding their money back. Who from? You first, and then us. As we have the same address and telephone number, they always catch up with us and let us know about your little problems – and they couldn't care less about causing family rows. They're right, of course. They want their money and they generally get it.

In these circumstances why do so many parents submit to this blackmail? Because they have no choice. Ever since you got your majority at eighteen, you've hardly needed to have anything – just a few pounds – in order to get a cheque book. Naturally the banks are on their guard, but if you take the precaution of giving the same address as Mummy or Daddy, the process is simple . . . child's play.

That is, until the day when we've finally had enough and we tell you we'll bale you out, but we're cutting off your allowance. Before going to such extremes we have been diddled by you right, left and centre.

3. Re-allocation of funds

When you've got holes in your socks or ladders in your tights, what do you do? Throw them in the dustbin and tell us that you can't possibly walk around in the middle of winter barefoot.

When your son or daughter asks for money to keep his/her feet warm, what can you do? You take a note out of your purse and hand it to the poor little barefoot child.

That would be fine if the note didn't frequently get deflected from its intended destination. Two pairs of socks or tights are roughly the equivalent of two cinema seats, hamburgers for three, a gallon or two of petrol for a penniless schoolfriend or two-thirds of a cassette. Sometimes two pairs of socks aren't the equivalent of anything at all: a few coins in the bottom of a pocket which just disappear, or a couple of Cokes and cigarettes all round. Nothing to write home about. So why make such a fuss about two pairs of socks when all we're asking is one note to replace the one which inadvertently got frittered away. Parents are really mean.

The way you re-allocate money we have given you for basic essentials to satisfy your own ends drives us mad. It can't be called theft, but it's misappropriation of private funds. You take advantage of our willingness to 'clothe the needy' in order to extract from us small but often repeated amounts, which you then spend exactly as you like.

Sometimes this abuse of trust is used to cover larger sums, usually where clothes are concerned. Instead of something essential like a raincoat you buy a sleeveless pullover, or a leather skirt instead of a pair of trousers; sometimes you spend our money on red shoes with three inch heels, and not on the dark blue, sensible walking shoes for which it was intended. I suppose I'm lucky if you don't blow the whole of your allowance on one sweater ('but it's cashmere') or on a single pair of shoes ('but they'll last me at least ten years').

We parents find this business of clothes particularly difficult to control. You taught us very early on that **we should never buy anything for you if you weren't there yourselves**. One or two brand new things left hanging, unworn, in the clothes cupboard were enough to make us realise that only you could choose your own style. Anything we buy is absolutely out, money out of the window. So, when you go clothes-shopping, we just have to hand you the money even though we may totally disapprove of the way you spend it. In the long run this system seems less ridiculous than leaving brand-new clothes hanging in a cupboard.

4. Selling for nothing what cost us a fortune

Recently, selling possessions one no longer wants has become something of a national habit. Secondhand shops selling every kind of goods are multiplying: men's, women's and children's clothes, furniture, bric-a-brac etc. But nothing for young people. This missing category is easily explained: the secondhand market flourishes between you and covers an unbelievably wide range of commodities.

Sadly, as there are no rules, some buyers behave in a shockingly unethical way. Cameras, stereo sets, motor bikes, or sports equipment are sold off for a song. The proceeds of this secondhand sale never seem to get back to the original purchaser – US. It is pocketed and immediately spent by the nominal owner – YOU.

That's how these belongings which we had paid a fortune for disappear from your cupboards. Since you absolutely insisted they were vital necessities when you made us buy them, no doubt they will have to be replaced sooner or later. This is the sort of conversation that takes place two weeks before Christmas or Easter:

'Where are your ski boots? I've looked for them everywhere and I can't find them.'

'You know quite well that I sold them to Stephen last year.'

(I need hardly add that 'you know quite well . . .' is one of the younger generation's common phrases when questioned about anything. He had quite definitely not told anyone, particularly his mother, about his little exploit. Selling off a virtually new pair of ski boots for fifteen pounds is scarcely something to be proud of.)

'What d'you mean, sold? You're mad, they weren't even two years old. You needn't think that I'm going to buy you another pair!'

But that's just what he does think. And, in fact, he's right. Unless, of course, one makes do with hiring a pair, which is hardly an economic solution, although it does have the advantage of preventing their untimely resale.

It's not easy to find work.

All this chicanery is depressing for today's parents. Since we wanted to encourage you to be financially responsible, we decided that we would give you a set amount of pocket money, weekly at first and then monthly. All the magazines recommended this method: 'Teach your children the value of money. Let them spend their money as they like – they will learn how much things cost and will find out how to economise and even how to save. Then, when they grow up they will be in a better position to manage their budget and cope with their money problems.'

My job, when you were at school, was writing for magazines. So, more than anyone, I approved of these modern teaching methods. As a modern woman I didn't want to have absolute power of control over the distribution of cash. The way the weekly housekeeping allowance was handed to our grandmothers by distrustful husbands who were afraid their money would be frittered away if they gave away too much at a time seems to me thoroughly outdated. I was all for personal bank accounts for women even if they had no earnings of their own. I therefore had to agree that, logically, young people should be granted some financial independence. I believed absolutely that people only learn to manage by being managers.

So each month I gave you an overall sum which was to cover ALL your expenses. I worked out that this amount would be quite enough to prevent you being broke by the twentieth of each month. And yet, however generous I was in my calculations, there was never enough cash to cover your expenses. In fact, because of continued borrowing, your overdraft became chronic, and our financial discussions more and more stormy.

Having been let down by you so many times, I began to lose confidence in my system. Very soon I had to face facts: trust does not necessarily lead to responsibility. It makes me sad to have to admit it.

If I didn't want to act as Paymaster General there was only one solution: to have a complete break. I would have to stop your allowance and tell you to support yourself by taking odd jobs.

Easier said than done. The American system of working students is an ideal way of coping with the changeover from dependence to complete self-reliance. The list of possible jobs is endless: baby-sitters, petrol pump attendants, errand boys (or girls), temporary office workers, temporary sales assistants, etc. But are these jobs always obtainable in practice?

The recent economic crisis didn't help when it came to persuading you to go out and earn some money. In the first place, you weren't exactly keen to go and look for work, and secondly it was almost impossible for you to find a job. I say 'for you to find' but actually we were the ones who had to slog our guts out, ringing round all our friends and relations. After replying to two or three ads without getting anywhere, you just gave up the whole thing.

And here is one I just happened to come across today when I was writing this:

'Publishing house seeks young men or women, preferably students, prepared to sell on foot, to distribute a widely advertised report. Reasonable commission to be paid each evening.' Then the address and telephone number. We can hardly begrudge the fact that you're not mugs enough to be taken in by this 'reasonable commission'.

When the children give up, the parents start looking. I have met two indefatigable women who finally found something, after making numerous telephone calls. They both used the Yellow Pages.

Joanna was determined to get her son, David, a summer job with a market gardener. She hated the idea of his spending all the holidays cooped up in an office or shop – he already looked off colour after a very bad winter and extremely bad school marks. She and her husband had threatened David with having to spend the whole summer working if he failed his exams to get into the final year at school. So, in order to carry out this threat, she felt she really had to find him a job as an assistant gardener.

'My husband is a surveyor and I work in the rag trade, so I'd never met a market gardener in my life. I felt that all I could do was bluff my way through. There are seventy-two market gardens in the local telephone directory, and it took me thirty-nine calls before finding anyone to show the faintest interest. In the end I found one who was prepared to see him on condition that I went along myself one evening before dinner. It was right the other side of town, and I had to leave work three hours early to be a sort of employment agent for my son, dealing with the owner of the nursery who looked uncooperative to say the least. I don't know what he thought of my son, but I must have made a good impression on him: he got the job.'

David pulled up leeks and planted lettuces for minimum wages for two months. It seems to have given him a very different view of life at school.

Sally's case is different. It wasn't a question of punishing her, but of helping her. When meeting a potential employer she was paralysed with shyness, and she was quite incapable of answering an advertisement by telephone. In order to find her a job as trainee beautician, her mother systematically went down the list of all the beauty salons in their nearest large town. After spending an average of two hours on the telephone each day for a whole week, she finally managed to get her taken on for a month, for tips only. Sally and her mother reckoned it was a lot better than nothing. It's no good expecting too much in these days of unemployment!

Sometimes you're actually able to earn a bit of money because a friend's sister gets married and you act as chauffeur to the bride, or your neighbour's aunt hires you for a couple of weeks as assistant in her beauty shop. Or you may even be asked to invigilate at an exam – but, at the pace you live at, these occasional earnings are just a drop in the ocean. So we can't really cut you off, even though we regularly threaten to do so.

In fact it's not till much later, and then for your own good rather than for the sake of our finances, that we will decide to do it, and we will return to this moment later on. For now, we will confine ourselves to saying that our fine principles of self-management and sharing have not proved successful when applied to our children's financial training.

And there are plenty of other areas where our liberal upbringing has produced results which are questionable to say the least. Studies is one of them.

VI

I've Never Been A Kyoiku-Mama

I'm sorry – I've never been a Kyoiku-mama.

This subject has been on my mind ever since I read an article explaining that Japanese mothers can take nearly all the credit for the astonishing technological and industrial success of their country.

Little Seiji Hashimoto, aged ten, isn't working well in class and he is likely to be expelled. Being bad students in Japan is no laughing matter – they get thrown out. The dishonour of such an expulsion distresses Seiji's mother so much that she gets ill. Psychosomatic or not, Seiji feels guilty – his mother's illness is his fault. To help her get better, Seiji makes great efforts at school – his marks improve and his mother recovers.

Californian researchers, trying to discover if the reasons for Japan's boom have roots in their culture, have reported hundreds of similar stories. Everywhere they have revealed the same pattern: mothers, fanatically concerned about their children's education, are prepared to apply every kind of psychological pressure, including emotional blackmail, to make them study and pass their exams.

The more interfering and demanding they are, the more their children (or should we say their sons?) achieve. These Japanese mothers feel so personally responsible for marks and class order that they arrange extra coaching in the evenings with professional tutors. Occasionally they go too far, and some children crack up: Japan has the highest school-age suicide rate in the world. But, in spite of these 'accidents', no one questions the system which mass-produces the best maths and science students in the world.

An international association for evaluating educational standards tested the scientific knowledge of pupils between 10 and 15 in the world's fifteen most industrialised countries. The Japanese came first on all counts. At the age of 10 their average mark was 5 points ahead of the others; at 15 the gap had widened: the Japanese were 9 points ahead. In these tests the scores of the American students were similar to those of other nationalities.

These results gave rise to concern in American university circles accustomed to their country's pre-eminence in the scientific domain. They sought explanations. Several years of research and enquiry in the Far East showed that there were two essential points of difference:

1. **The number of school days each year.** Japanese pupils spend **240** days at school each year, American children **178.** The figure for Great Britain is **200.** In this respect the French come last: their children spend only **149** days at school each year!

I cannot help thinking that this low rating has some bearing on academic standards. Not so much where actual knowledge is concerned – and a child can only absorb so much – as in the place that work occupies in the individual's daily life. When you are used to working less than one day in two, starting regular daily employment must seem really punishing. Doing nothing is more 'normal' than working. This no doubt explains the unreliability of so many young people in the private sector. All employers complain of apprentices and trainees disappearing when the summer holidays begin.

2. **Maternal involvement.** This factor is all the more important as Japanese women give up work immediately they marry and take little part in social life which is mainly the province of business men. Mothers therefore tend to justify their existence through their children's success. And since Japanese families are small, maternal pressure is all the greater for being concentrated on fewer children.

In Japan, mothers of good students bear the proud name of *kyoiku-mama*, which can be roughly translated as 'education mother', though this definition doesn't cover her exclusive devotion to one single task: to make her child the best pupil in the class.

The anthropologist George de Vos, of the University of California at Berkeley, has been studying Japanese culture for twenty-five years. He says of the *kyoiku-mama:* 'Japanese mothers can be considered today's equivalent of the world's best "Jewish mother".'

A Harvard psychologist gives his comparison: 'Until her son starts school, the Japanese mother devotes herself entirely to bringing up her little boy. By her words and actions she lets him know the whole time how much she loves him, and that for her he is the most important thing in the world. Then she says to him, "After all I've done for you, don't let me down." Like the Jewish mother who says, "How can you say you're not hungry when I've slaved over a hot stove all day to get this meal ready for you?" '

Traditional Jewish mothers raise a laugh in plays because of their extravagant emotions, but the essential part they play in the cultural development of their people is recognised nevertheless. All this energy and effusiveness were needed to persuade so many little Jewish children to stay cooped up for hours with the rabbi learning Hebrew sacred verses – otherwise they would have been out playing with other children.

Talking about this sort of thing, do you know the difference between the three main types of Jewish and Christian mothers? Three little boys go to school together: one French, one Italian and one Jewish. In the afternoon they come home and give their reports to their mothers – they have come bottom of the class.

The French mother says severely: 'You should be ashamed of yourself, my son. How are you going to get anywhere in life with marks like that? I'm warning you, if you go on like this **you will destroy yourself**!'

The Italian mother starts shouting: 'My son, your results are terrible. I can't bear to see you ruin your life like this.

I would rather be dead than see you make a mess of things. I'm warning you, if you go on like this **I will destroy myself**!'

The Jewish mother wails: 'My son, your marks prove you don't love me. How could you have done so badly after all my efforts and all the sacrifices I have made since you were born so that you could go to school? I'm warning you, if you go on like this **you will destroy me**!'

The French obsession with qualifications

This is approved of by French parents. Where scholastic requirements are concerned, the system has stood up quite well in France since about the beginning of this century. It wasn't so much a matter of learning in order to acquire knowledge as of studying in order to succeed. We had one of the best educational systems for producing graduates. Once he had got his degree, the graduate could rest on his laurels for the rest of his professional life. This craze for qualifications has not completely disappeared in the protected areas of our national economy. In research and industry, both exposed to international competition, graduates discover that they now have to push themselves hard both to get started in the first place, and to keep their position afterwards, but in certain branches of administration an official scroll is enough to guarantee thirty or forty years' automatic promotion.

A young graduate joining French Railways from the Ecole des Hautes Etudes Commerciales, (HEC), the famous Paris business school, cannot expect to earn the same salary as a graduate who joins at the same time from the Ecole Polytechnique, the oldest and grandest of the French educational establishments. Only by gross incompetence could the Polytechnique graduate fail to get to the top, thus allowing the HEC graduate to catch him up. Otherwise, in spite of making a tremendous effort and getting good results, the HEC graduate, as holder of an inferior degree, will earn less until the day he retires.

In order to compete in this rat race, the French

educational system, which includes at least four vital qualifying exams, students had to have their heads crammed with things that hardly equipped them for the outside world. Rather than being allowed to develop their minds, children were made to stuff them as full of facts as possible; the idea of this was to make selection easier as the fullest brains were considered the best.

This force-feeding resulted in a super-charged memory at the expense of other intellectual faculties. Almost everything had to be learnt by heart: multiplication tables, irregular verbs, the hundred years war, the plays of Shakespeare, the counties of England, the rules of Latin grammar, mathematical theorems and formulae, figures for coal production, Kings of England, etc . . . !

Ninety-nine per cent of what we learnt was totally useless. But the remaining one per cent formed a sort of collective culture. Even those parents whose academic attainments have been overtaken by their children can impress them by remembering, years after they left school, that 'accommodation' has two m's and that 7 x 8 has always made 56, with or without a calculator, and always will.

Above all, this system made it possible for mothers to take an active part in their children's lives and academic achievements. All they had to do, every evening, was to listen to them reciting what was written in the textbook. Learning by heart avoided misunderstandings and differences of interpretation which could arise between what the child heard at school and what he was told at home.

Mothers kept their eyes firmly on the school reports and class position and were convinced that too much time off was bad for results. They made up for the idleness of the long summer months by imposing daunting holiday work on their children and, obsessed by the idea of getting them into a first-class university, they made them do maths lessons rather than go swimming – they would excuse them from sport without a second thought, but would send them off to take maths or physics exams even if they were shivering with a high temperature. There was little to choose between European mothers and their Japanese opposite numbers.

Fathers aided and abetted them in their capacity as acting prefects, always chipping in: 'Let's see your exercise book. That's very good – here's some extra pocket money', or 'That's not very good. No cinema/television/party/Sunday outing for you next weekend'. And even today some overworked businessmen ease their consciences in a matter of moments with a quick 'look at the exercise book'. Once they have made this gesture they can bury themselves in their files again, or relax in front of the television. Children know very well that academic results are no joking matter.

Happy children=better pupils

When we became parents everything went topsy-turvy. Good old-fashioned teaching methods were under attack on all sides. Just as the Americans are wondering today what it is that makes Japanese students so successful, we ourselves made a study of American scientists' childhoods to try and find out how they managed to send men on to the moon who hadn't been either bribed or punished when they were small.

Modernists such as myself recommended active teaching methods, participation in class, group work, oral work, modern maths and A.S. Neill's *Summerhill*. We were convinced that happy children would be better pupils. They must acquire a taste for understanding rather than be forced to learn.

Between the Sixties and the Eighties, therefore, away went: dictation exercises, learning geographical regions or dates by heart, marking from 1–20 (replaced by the much less precise A, B, C, D), class positions, homework, detention, mental arithmetic, Latin, history of dates, re-taking failed exams, prize-giving and two levels of school-leaving exams. (Distinctions in the higher school-leaving examination and in national scholarship examinations nearly got thrown out too, in the drive to eliminate competition, but were brought back at the last moment; the educational pendulum has begun to swing back again, and some people are beginning to rediscover that good results produce motivation.)

The peak moment of this upheaval took place just after the 'cultural revolution' of May 1968. 'Set fire to the schoolbooks . . . burn the teachers too . . .' The great dream of our restricted childhood was to be realised for our children. How wonderful!'

Relationships between parents and children became much simpler. Parents no longer needed to supervise their children's homework when they got back from the office. Children in junior school virtually had no homework, and anything the older children brought home was nowadays quite beyond the parents' capacities. In maths and physics for instance, everything had changed since their day. Even the French Revolution was no longer what it had been: it had just become part of the general pageant of history, and the storming of the Bastille in July 1789 or Christopher Columbus discovering America in 1492 were no more than chapter headings.

I'll always remember the primary school teacher who implored us, during a parents' evening, 'Above all, never teach them that two and two make four or they'll never understand modern maths!'

Like the other mothers, there was nothing else I could do after that, except have confidence in you and hope that these revolutionary studies, which on the whole seemed more intelligent than those we had been made to follow, would awaken in you a thirst for knowledge which is essential if anything worthwhile is to be achieved. I was proud that we were going to be part of this rapid development of a new kind of youthful intellect, more creative and original, and better adapted to this century that we had ever been.

To be absolutely honest, I should add that this arrangement fitted in beautifully with my timetable as a working woman. All I needed to do was to supervise English or natural science essays. I could manage this as lists of verbs and biological diagrams haven't altered too much since I studied them.

That is how, because of changes which I myself had wished for, I gave up trying to be a Japanese mother.

I am puzzled by the results.

You speak atrociously

When I try to compare your knowledge with mine at the same age – it has to be the same age of course, or the comparison wouldn't make sense at all – I feel uneasy.

For instance, I find it extremely irritating that you are incapable of writing two lines without making a grammatical or spelling mistake, usually both at the same time. It's irritating, but I don't think it's too serious. There are enough proof readers and office dictionaries to correct or prevent the worst mistakes. Most of you will not become professional writers. I would willingly overlook a few spelling mistakes, if in spite of not knowing how to write you could just manage to speak properly.

But, oh dear, you speak atrociously!

I don't mean slang. You're perfectly entitled to have fun with your secret languages. We had ours, why shouldn't you have yours? Each generation has a right to its own secret language. But, when we weren't using our particular slang, we spoke properly. You don't.

Your everyday speech is nothing but a series of unintelligible sounds, abbreviated swear words and truncated expressions. Anyone would think that talking made you so tired that you swallow half the words to save yourself the effort of pronouncing them.

If you want to know my opinion, it's fun to do this sort of thing at thirteen, usual at fifteen, silly at eighteen and idiotic at twenty. As is the case with sticking to a timetable, or organising yourself properly, the way you speak must begin to have some relation with the outside world. You won't be spending the rest of your life surrounded by a gang of inarticulate chums.

I've got another theory which is more optimistic: you

know perfectly well how to speak properly; the proof is that you managed to pass your A-levels and to begin, and sometimes to continue, higher education. But you deliberately carry on talking gibberish in front of us and amongst yourselves just to prolong your adolescent way of communicating. This rejection of adult language surely tells us a lot about your mentality. Instead of giving you the urge to progress and discover, to change the world and make revolutions, to introduce your own ideas and culture, and demolish ours, your studies have left you in a sort of adolescent cocoon, snug and isolated in your own world, completely out of touch with the reality of today and the demands of tomorrow.

In fact, I can see very well what your education has lacked in comparison with ours: a whole jumble of facts and rules which stifle the spirit without necessarily firing the imagination. But I'm still trying to find out what *more* you have learnt.

You don't know how to write a letter longer than three lines, but neither have you learnt how to dictate your ideas or conclusions into a recording machine.

You've never had to rebel at copying out pages of neat handwriting, but neither have you been made to learn how to use a keyboard – absolutely vital for your existence in the technological world of tomorrow.

You're not taught your country's history any more, but neither have you begun to learn what is going on in the rest of the world, past or present.

You don't learn Latin any more, but neither do you study Basic or Pascal languages to dialogue with a computer.

We knew hardly any foreign languages when we left school, and nor do you.

Our musical and physical education simply didn't exist. You have made a very modest start.

Let's be clear about this: I don't say we were perfect, far from it. I have no wish for you to be like me at your age, I would have liked you to be **better.** More enlightened, more open, more original, more enterprising, more everything.

I would have liked you to astonish me but, disappointingly, I'm not impressed.

A creative generation

And yet, there is one area for which I admire you, a quality which I acknowledge and on which I base much hope: creativity.

Liberal and unrestricted education, with its flexible syllabuses, positive methods and encouragement of enterprise, has given us a generation of artists, acrobats, fashion designers, advertising experts, singers, photographers, radio presenters, dancers and cartoonists. One needs only to observe who your heroes are to understand your dearest ambition: to express your talents rather than develop your abilities.

It is better than nothing, but still not enough for the modern world. Without manufacturing and trade, without technicians and managers, your fine creativity is unlikely to keep you indefinitely in the latest comforts. If imagination is all that matters to you, and to hell with effort, efficiency and drive, then you're heading for disaster, my friends!

By striving to give you what we lacked most, we may have done you a really bad turn. As we had too much work, we decreased yours, but not ours. This is a fatal mistake – you should make great efforts when you're young because it's only then that you're capable of learning everything. Just as East German athletes go in for serious competition from the moment they get to primary school, so the brain needs to be trained to extend itself.

The anthropologist Claude Levi-Strauss was courageous enough to say so on the television. He inveighed against mankind's increasing tendency to condone childish behaviour: 'I believe in compulsion in education. Montaigne learnt Latin when he was five or six.'

That's what I told you. Watching you let slip all the fantastic learning opportunities available to you, I really begged you to apply yourself, but I believe it was probably already too late. A taste for learning can't be taught, it comes from long habit and by constant and firm pressure. A child has to get from his background the feeling that he must push himself and do well for the sake of his parents.

I certainly never was a Japanese mother. In my defence it must be admitted that, to back me up over this educational policy, I didn't have either a Japanese husband, Japanese school teachers, Japanese university professors or Japanese politicians.

For the last twenty years, society has on the whole concerned itself with the lot of teachers and somewhat neglected the students. And unless you change the one you can't modify the other. The teachers themselves are aware of this, and one can foresee that there will be some movement in years to come. But that will affect your children's generation, not you.

It's too late now to turn you into a little Japanese. There's only one teacher who can sort you out, and that's you yourself. Good luck to him! He's going to have to teach you so much that we left out!

Anyhow, now that you're nearly grown up, my educational role has ended. I feel very guilty about this when I know that you're not prepared to make use of all the wonderful opportunities that are open to you. When I think of all the young people who would give anything to be able to continue their studies but have to give up for financial reasons, your couldn't-care-less attitude really shocks me. There are thousands of parents like us who are willing to finance your years of higher education, but not if you end up in second-rate universities or colleges, and then give up your degree course.

'Laziness is the mother of vices,' my grandmother used to say, and she was **ABSOLUTELY RIGHT.**

Now I'm beginning to preach, which is what you hate. I only need to see your expression the moment I turn to you and say 'I want to have a word with you' – the dreaded phrase which you know perfectly well means I'm going to give you a lecture on my boring opinion about the purpose of life.

'But please listen, all the same: I want to have a word with you . . .'

VII

You Can't Do Just As You Like

'Absolutely thrilling, Mum.' This is your way of showing me that you have no intention of continuing a discussion which you consider desperately boring.

'Absolutely thrilling' means that what I'm trying to say to you in the fairest way possible doesn't interest you in the slightest. When I was young we used to say, 'Carry on talking, I'm listening . . .' At least, we said it sotto voce, not daring to say it out loud to our parents when they were lecturing us. I think in that respect you are better than we were – at least you're frank, perhaps even cynical, in your opinions.

'Absolutely thrilling, Mum!' How scornful you are about what I think – I'm only trying to hand on some of my ideas and experience. You're totally indifferent to my idiotic opinions about learning, effort, respect for other people and the restrictions of living in a community. You just refuse to see any connection between making an effort when you're young and getting somewhere when you're grown up.

Put like that, it does sound a bit like a lesson in civic responsibilities, I agree. Faced with your indifference, I sometimes wonder if you're pretending not to understand, or if you're deliberately not listening to my little homily on good and evil.

I am very conscious of the glib kind of moralising to which I so objected during the height of my own adolescent rebellion, and therefore I make a big effort not to be heavy-handed, and to make constructive suggestions rather than lay down the law. I find that setting a good example is better than ordering you about.

Oh dear, the GOOD EXAMPLE! That's what you have to give to your little brother. It's also what stops you leaning your elbows on the table, and is used by one or other grown-up as an excuse for exercising absolute tyranny in the household. Poor Daddy, the number of times he got scolded for picking his nose in case we should copy him. Parents in those days were absolutely bedevilled by the GOOD EXAMPLE – they regarded it in the same way as women did their DUTY. No lying in in the mornings, no casual clothes, no swearing in public, no quarrelling in front of the children, and no show of affection. You behaved in a very upright fashion.

Obviously my way of setting a GOOD EXAMPLE is a bit different. It's more relaxed and less conventional. I quite often swear mildly, give my man a kiss and don't mind being seen with nothing on. I think relationships are more important; for instance if you want other people to be nice to you, you'd better start by being nice to them. It's much better to discuss things than to make an awful face and sulk. You can't always go on asking for things and give nothing in return. On the surface, that seems very different to what our parents taught us but, underneath, I think a lot of it is the same, everything depends on one's relationships being more or less satisfactory – within oneself first of all and secondly with other people.

It's on this particular point that our opinions differ widely and constantly. What shocks me doesn't bother you, and what horrifies me, you consider normal.

In these conditions it's not easy to come to terms with each other's life style and way of looking at things. We don't share a common ethical sense.

Trying to find a moral code

You're amazed that I should talk about ethics. It's not an expression that has ever been used in family conversation, only in philosophy classes at school. How can ethics come into remonstrances about domestic and financial matters? Since when did your mother bother her head about ethics?

Since you were born, I promise you. Ever since I took on the responsibility of bringing you into the world, I have been asking myself how I would help you to develop your character, and equip yourself to make the most of your life. Not necessarily a life like my own, which was the aim of parents in days gone by, but the sort of life you really want to lead, where you fully realise your potential.

Education can't exist without ethics, but for parents of my generation, these have been particularly tricky and difficult to define.

As children of the second world war we were able to question without destroying. The rules and values of pre-war society had disintegrated unaided, and we had the responsibility of creating new ones. Faced with the growth of the modern world and material comforts on the one hand, and the collapse of religion and middle-class values on the other, we had to grope our way towards a new lifestyle and moral code suitable for these novel circumstances.

What should be preserved from the teachings of Christian tradition? Which rules remain unchanged down the centuries because they are part of man's essential nature? What moral progress could be expected from scientific progress? Do social upheavals bring about changes in human nature? We have thoroughly examined the principles of our youth, sorted through them and drawn up a list of those which we considered indispensable, necessary, preferable, or useless and harmful, and have tried to bring you up on that basis, with all the inconsistencies that these changing values have given rise to in your education.

Some still believe in firmness and restrictions. Others, including myself, preferred flexibility and discussion. Modern teaching methods inspired by Freynet or Piaget gave little children the opportunity to develop without being subjected to the rules of grown-ups who were inevitably 'corrupted' by the restrictions of life in society and 'neurotic' as a result of the constraints of their own upbringing. Rousseau, the free thinker, getting his own back on Queen Victoria, in fact.

Parents' lives were frequently interrupted by violent differences of opinion over education. How many domestic rows have been caused in this way? And, when a couple's marriage has broken down, how often have they cited as reasons for the breakdown their profound disagreement over the meaning of life and what of importance should be handed on to future generations?

When couples are divorced, and don't have domestic rows because they're not living together any more, mutual reproaches about how the children are being brought up smoulder on for years.

'You're spoiling the boy – you'll turn him into a good-for-nothing!'

'You're too strict with the girl – you'll turn her into a rebel!'

Sometimes these clashes between your father and mother took place in front of you. You're not silly, you take advantage of these battles and get the more liberal of the two to take your side. As a rule, it's the more easy-going parent who gets the upper hand, as popular opinion prefers dangling a carrot. Without being completely free and easy like the Americans, we have become considerably more open-minded than we used to be.

In any case, you're not told the same thing by everyone any more. When the whole family was together, grandparents would say things categorically while parents only hinted.

At school, most teachers tended to be somewhat left-wing while others were more conservative. In the playground, when you compared your knowledge of adult life, you discovered that you were growing up in a world full of contradictions.

This diversity had its positive aspects – it gave you an early opportunity to develop your critical faculties. Whereas propaganda shapes the intellect in order to make everyone fit into an overall plan, an excess of knowledge allows you to use your judgment and encourages you to be non-conformist. At least one can say that you haven't had a conformist education.

The first generation of the sexual revolution

Let's take an example, surely the most spectacular one concerning young people over the age of fifteen: adolescent sexuality. In this area, fundamental to Christian morality, there has been a complete change in the space of twenty years. What used to be wrong has become the norm. The figures prove it: according to an opinion poll in the magazine *L'Etudiant* in 1983 78% of girls and 97% of boys in secondary schools had their first experience of sex before the age of nineteen.

Twenty-two per cent of girls still virgins at nineteen, you think that's a lot? I don't, not when I think back twenty or thirty years, when women of my generation were young.

A poll taken in March 1984 for a news magazine by professional public opinion researchers shows us how far we have come:

QUESTION: *How old were you when you had your first experience of sex?*

Women now aged	% under 15	% 15 – 16	% 17 – 18
50 – 64	–	–	12
35 – 49	–	5	10
25 – 34	2	10	30
18 – 24	4	21	37

Even the most conservative elements have had to accept this revolution. You now have full rights over your own body.

Thanks to who? Really, have you ever thought about it? You have taken on this freedom as if it were the most natural thing in the world. And yet it is truly thanks to us, your mothers, who fought to overcome the prohibitions which spoilt a substantial part of our own youth.

Did you know that the law permitting the use of the pill and contraception in France dated from December 1967? And that abortion was legalised in January 1975? Both became legal after you were already born, not so very long ago.

You are the first generation of the sexual revolution. We are happy that we were able to give you this fine new liberty for your sixteenth birthday. We even envied you for being born into a world where the Pill exists, where parents make sure that you take it, and where the Department of Education provides sex education lessons in secondary schools. Perhaps you do not fully appreciate the enormous advances in opinion which have made it possible for you to benefit from **all** aspects of being young.

An education adviser in a Paris Lycée stated recently: 'The students are very sweet, they greet each other with a kiss every morning. It is true that they have to cope with emotional problems, break-ups that hurt; sometimes they fall deeply in love while they are still at school. They confide in me a lot – a final year pupil told me this morning that he had failed because his girl-friend had finished with him.'

You are not particularly astonished at such a statement. But I am. I try and imagine the look on my headmistress's face if I had stood up in front of her, at the age of seventeen, and tried to explain that I had missed school because my love affair had broken up. I cannot begin to describe what her reaction would have been!

What fantastic freedom you have nowadays to play at love, as the Italians say, at the same age as Romeo and Juliet; without shame or reproaches.

Don't be so pompous

But endeavour needs more than permission, and success more than effort. This has been easily demonstrated by your red eyes, your emotional upheavals, your overdue periods.

Your casual attitude to contraception worries us. Birth

control had given us so much hope, but we see our daughters neglect it through irresponsibility, or fail to practise it through ignorance. We find ourselves begging you to take advantage of such progress.

We realise now that we were so busy opening up new pathways, that we failed to stress some of the basic guidelines for life in unknown territory.

This is where ethics come in again.

In sexual matters, for example, it should have been a matter of basic necessity to make quite clear that you are free to make love, the sexual act nowadays being accepted as a matter for the two partners involved, but you must have mutual respect for one another.

I've never used such high-flown language when talking to you, that's true. I would no doubt have felt very pompous, and you would have thought me quite ridiculous.

More than that, surely parents are the last people in the world you want to discuss love with. They don't discuss their love life with anyone else – they keep it to themselves, just as you do.

Parents used to be there to say no; all the sex education they could hand out consisted of negatives. Boys had to be warned and girls had to be kept safe. Now that they don't say no any more, they say nothing at all. It's as if they hadn't the courage yet awhile to change their stance from one of repression to one of forbearance. So much so that your so-called liberated childhood was surrounded by an embarrassed silence over everything to do with emotional or sexual problems. We couldn't find suitable words to deal with this new morality.

How do you explain the subtle borderlines between the erotic and the pornographic, between grand passion and fondness and between the kind of love that makes you wildly happy and the kind that makes you miserable, to young people who have scarcely begun to discover that wonderful and dangerous world of love and desire?

In order to discuss it we would have needed to feel sure of ourselves, which we weren't. It was all we could do to absorb these new moral standards into our own lives; we hadn't had enough experience to be able to share them with you. Converting the Christian tradition into the sexual revolution wasn't easy. We were too afraid that you would make fun of us and our good intentions.

So you see, I wonder now whether we were wrong to be afraid of being laughed at – whether or not we were over prudish in avoiding giving you those guidelines. They might not have done you any good, but they might have stopped you getting hurt, or hurting other people.

We were so proud of offering you a world that was more open and rich than it had been when we were young that we forgot to warn you about restrictions and obligations. Optimism was the reason for this failure in us. It wasn't enough to whet your appetite and encourage your talents, we should also have indicated limits and marked out boundaries.

Unfortunately, you can't do just as you like.

There are certain rules which you must respect. If you don't respect them, you can be sure that life will teach you a lesson.

Perhaps it's not too late to wave the red flag? It's said that you learn nothing from your parents' experience and that only your own setbacks and disappointments teach you about life. I wonder if that's really true.

How can you define in a few words the moral code of anyone's life? I have tried to find a basis on which I could sum up the essential parts. Why not the Ten Commandments? Which Ten Commandments, you ask. No, not Cecil B. de Mille's film, I mean the ones which God handed down to Moses on Mount Sinai, to sort things out a bit down here on earth. People used to learn them in Sunday school – I still know them off by heart, but you don't. It's hardly surprising as you've never learnt anything by heart – no poetry, or spelling lists. And no Ten Commandments either.

Still, let's try and see what message, as the advertising people would say, the Ten Commandments are trying to put across, and whether the message is still valid in modern society. Don't worry, it won't take long – we'll soon get through it.

The first three Commandments are concerned with God. We'll put them on one side. My own ideas on the subject are so precise and so personal that I decided long ago that I would never preach my agnostic crusade. Contrary to what religious believers think, it is even more difficult to define one's moral code if God does not come into it – but that's another story, and this book does not claim to be a treatise on metaphysics. No precise instruction, then, on commandments one, two and three.

Equally, let us ignore numbers six and nine. They condemn, in the most absolute terms, lust and other sins of the flesh outside the bonds of marriage. We have just agreed that morals have changed radically in this particular area.

That leaves the other five. All very relevant.

The fourth urges filial love as a guarantee of long life: which is what this book is very much about. We will come back to it.

As for the remaining four, they deal with: murder, violence, theft, respect for others and concern for the truth. Everything which divides barbarism from civilisation. Everything which causes us such anguish when we realise how easily our more or less civilised society could be dragged down and engulfed – this western culture as we have always known it is far from perfect but, compared to others, still remarkably fit to live in.

Don't let these four commandments fall into disuse. You would be the first victims of a return to barbarism, and your future really depends on you alone.

Disagreement over property

Let us take an example: respect for property. It surprised me that two commandments out of ten in the Tables of the Law – twenty per cent of the message – dealt with this subject. Surely that is a lot? Almost as many as those dealing with the Lord, and equal to those concerned with lust. It must have been particularly difficult to make

progress in that aspect of primitive society in the Nea
East.

Is theft more 'natural' than honesty? Whatever the trut
of the matter, we only need to look at the behaviour o
your generation to realise that the problem is still wit
us.

In fact we disagree totally about the whole idea o
property. You boast about nicking things in shops, o
using public transport without paying, of climbing ove
the barrier on the Underground, of getting into the cinem
free through the exit, of possessing the biggest collectio
of 'borrowed' cigarette lighters or ballpoint pens, of swi
ching supermarket price labels and getting away with it a
the check-out.

It was from you that I learnt the foolproof way o
drinking the finest claret when you can't afford such luxu
wine. You pick the price label off a bottle of ordina
table wine, stick it on a bottle of a very special vintag
and put it in your trolley amongst all your other purchase
The check-out girl can't be expected to know the price o
every single item and is not necessarily a wine buff; sh
just gets on with her job and rings up the price shown o
the label. Pretty neat, don't you think?

No, I'm very sorry, I don't agree. First it's dishones
second it's stupid.

If everyone did it, life would be impossible. No mo
trade, no more shopping, no more community life o
commercial activity. Theft isn't just a dangerous spor
it's the breeding ground of anarchy.

It's only necessary to see your expressions when yo
yourselves are the victims to realise what a keen sens
you each have of your OWN property. Whoever pinche
something off your motor bike or old banger one nig
when you were in bed had better watch out! And th
same goes for the crook who filched the wallet out of yo
pocket when you were kipping on the train. If you cou
get hold of them, you'd really beat them up! And yet yo
are amazed at grown-ups who react in the same way whe
you make a sport out of thieving.

Actually, in most cases you nick things for a laug

ertainly not because you are in dire straits. I saw one of hese silly thefts in our local supermarket.

The young man was wearing ridiculously pointed owboy boots, and a good pair of jeans. A caricature of oung, idle unemployment, up-market version. There was o question of being driven to steal out of misery and unger. He was a beginner: the young cashier only had o ask him to undo his jacket as he came up to the till for im to go bright red in the face and start to run. A couple f security men caught him within a few yards – they ound two pre-packed slices of smoked salmon on him. o he was led off to the police station under the awkward aze of the customers. How many of them must have vondered, as I did, if it was really worth getting mixed p with the police for two slices of smoked salmon?

I felt sorry for this would-be cowboy. There was somehing pathetic about his wretched attempt at grabbing a it of luxury for himself. A hundred years ago people vere thrown into prison for taking bread; but now, when eople's standard of living has improved so much, they ardly ever steal in order to eat; they do it because they vant to snatch a moment's luxury, or share in a dream. Iow else can you explain the fact that thieves of your age ake sports cars, never family ones?

My sadness was a bit personal too. I couldn't help hinking that, but for the grace of God, it could have been ou being dragged off to the police station by those two ecurity men. All through your adolescence I dreaded a all from the police to say you had been caught doing a amn stupid thing – the only expression fit to describe the nnumerable petty crimes, more irritating than serious, hat you and your friends think up in order to show what nen' you are.

I've never been telephoned over a really serious matter.)nce I had to go and fetch you from a police station ecause you had gone to a rock concert with a bicycle hain in your mack pocket. Trust your luck – the police vere searching everyone as they went in to stop any armed ghts. They pushed you into their van with three others, ho'd got flick knives and a cosh. You swore to me that

your bicycle chain was purely for self defence, and w
didn't discuss it again. Your expression when I went int
the police station was enough to stop me going on abou
it.

I have no reason to be proud of your clean polic
record. You have always got away with it, and it's mor
by good luck than good judgment that you've never bee
had up in court. Fortunately, I think that you've no
given up these sort of escapades. It seems to me that yo
and your friends have got beyond petty theft, and hav
gradually got sick of violence. I don't hear anything thes
days about scraps on Saturday nights over bent bumpers
or getting your own back on someone who's insulted you

Perhaps getting a black eye one day made you begin t
understand – getting the worst of it put some sense int
your head.

It's a bit ridiculous to think that it took a sock in th
eye to make you see that we weren't always wrong t
warn you against violence, both yours and other people's

It's awful to find ourselves quite unable to communicat
with you – we would so like to help you avoid disasters
but we just have to look on in agony while you figh
your own battles. In fact, it's rather like having a boxin
champion for a son. (I can't think of anything worse tha
to be the mother of a boxer, and to have to accept tha
someone should make a profit out of hitting your son ove
the head!) We have to sit quietly at the ringside while yo
do silly things, and remain unmoved as we wait to se
whether you win or lose, and whether you turn out to b
a fighter, or find yourself handicapped for life becaus
you weren't strong or agile enough to defend yourself.

Others, your friends (your managers in this case), ar
allowed to advise you between rounds and give you a b
of friendly encouragement or point out your opponent'
weak points and how best you can attack or defend your
self. You listen to them, even if they know nothing abou
life and their advice isn't necessarily good.

As mothers, we feel every blow you get, right where
hurts, and all we're allowed to do is mind our own bus

ness. You don't trust our advice – you reject it because it's too soft.

Because of this I have usually thought it better to keep quiet rather than annoy you. But even then you told me I said too much.

On the other hand, I'm aware that there are many essential matters I myself haven't broached with you.

We should have been able to discuss everything I'm writing about now as part of our daily routine – it shouldn't have all come pouring out now, in a book. But we never found the time to talk frankly together about these all-important matters. You were too busy growing up and I was too engrossed in my own life to be aware of danger signals. We got into the bad habit of not talking to one another – I realise that now, and it's becoming clear to me **why** we don't understand each other.

VIII

The Family Circle In Perpetual Motion

One day I felt particularly low. I felt I couldn't go on being strong and cheerful any more. I felt quite disorientated and helpless, as though I might break down at any moment. I wished I had someone older than me to turn to for comfort – I just wanted to be someone's child instead of everyone's mother.

It was Sunday, and there were only the two of us in the house. You were unenthusiastically flicking through your usual batch of magazines and I was completing the typical working woman's tasks – the sort of paperwork that ruins a weekend because you've put off doing it during the week, official forms and monthly bills. I finished these boring tasks, but couldn't work up any enthusiasm over the television with its slick meaningless chat.

I felt the need to talk and discuss things – I wanted for once to share the weaker side of my character with you, to show you a different kind of mother, not as strong as I appear, whose problems in life aren't so different from yours. We're told time and time again that in order to look young we must look cheerful, but one would hardly think so if your frequent expressions of deep gloom were anything to go by. In spite of your firm cheeks and your unlined eyes, you smile less often than we do. Perhaps if we could just let ourselves go into depths of melancholy we might be able to get closer to you? Or rather, you might think us more like you?

If parents behaved less like grown-ups, would young people behave less like little children?

That's what I wanted to believe on that Sunday afternoon.

I suddenly felt quite overcome with misery. I let fall a tear – it's stupid, girls always cry and, whether I like it or not, I'm still a girl and always will be, and you looked at me absolutely horrified. I can sunbathe topless in front of you and it doesn't worry you at all, but crying – how frightfully embarrassing! I felt so awkward. Once I'd really let go I just couldn't stem the flow.

I tried to stammer out some feeble excuses: 'I'm tired' – 'I don't know what's come over me' – 'It's stupid to let myself go like that! I'm so depressed . . . you must understand what it's like at your age . . .' The more I tried to stop, the more I howled.

I hunted for a tissue and rushed to the cold water tap to bathe my red eyes. You looked so relieved that I had pulled myself together again. I tried to make a joke of the whole thing as I felt this was my only way out of such an embarrassing scene.

As I went up to my room, unbelievably it was you I felt sorry for. How awkward I must have made you feel!

Never again since then – it must be three years ago now – have I made the slightest attempt to let my hair down and talk to you as I did that time. Quite unable to throw off my classic 'mother-image' I've kept my little drama to myself. This film of my melancholy is not for showing to the under-twenties.

Your wall of silence

It's odd that one can't discuss anything with one's children even when they're old enough to share in other people's thoughts and problems. Other people's children will talk to you all right, but not your own.

Very often in professional life, a friend will telephone: 'Could you be very kind and have a word with my daughter? She doesn't seem to be able to organise her life, and I think it would be a great help to her to talk to someone outside the family.'

The girl turns up. She's intelligent, she listens well, is pleasant and polite and expresses herself with confidence. Suddenly you remember that her father described her as silent and shy, or stubborn and aggressive. The person in front of you has nothing in common with the father's description. Why is it our children are so uncommunicative with us and yet so open with other people?

A hospital psychiatrist told me one day about the rows he had with his nineteen-year-old daughter. She accused him of being jealous of her boyfriend and of being bad-tempered every time he came to collect her. She also told him he was hypocritical in not letting the boy visit her in her room. The whole situation was quite clear: in his professional capacity as a therapist, he would find such an attitude completely unacceptable coming from another father. The psychiatrist admitted that his daughter wasn't entirely wrong. How could this conflict be explained?

'You are right to show surprise. I have asked myself the same question, and I can only find one answer: no one can be both father and analyst at the same time. The "distancing" which is part of a professional consultation is entirely missing when it comes to dealing with my own family problems. I would really need to have a split personality to make our relationship impersonal. Not only does this seem difficult, but I'm not at all sure that it is what my daughter wants. No doubt she needs this confrontation to give herself confidence both in her own eyes and those of her boyfriend.'

How we sympathise with the psychiatrist's confusion. And how reassuring it is too for all those parents who have come up against the same silent barrier. Does this mean it's 'normal' not to be able to communicate with one's children?

Just because something is 'normal' doesn't mean it's necessarily acceptable. It's normal to want to hit people who annoy you, but that doesn't mean you should go ahead and do so. The main effort of civilisation concentrates on an attempt to improve our basic instincts and feelings, even if only a little. Do parents and children really have to talk to each other as though they belonged to different families?

In a remarkable book on couples, Jacques Salome poses questions on possible ways of improving communication between men and women. I felt that what he said could equally well apply to communication between parents and children:

> In order to establish a relationship you need more than just feelings: you need to get closer to one another and try to reconcile your differences. Feelings often depend on good communication for their existence.
>
> By making my position as clear as possible in a discussion I can improve my communication.
>
> You can only relieve your feelings by speaking your mind, however painful that may be. Ties of love are not enough to keep two people together – they need to communicate their fears and desires to one another.
>
> Thinking that a dialogue can be carried on automatically shows a lack of recognition of the constant misunderstandings and pitfalls that can be encountered.

These communication difficulties can be explained by the entrenched attitudes people take up. Parents and children dig in behind their traditional positions without paying enough heed to the changing attitudes and circumstances of modern society.

To find a new level we need to recognise new roles and firmly redefine the terms of the contract which binds us together. We have already learnt that this sort of readjustment is essential for a couple if they are to have any chance of living together successfully. Isn't it exactly the same for other members of the family circle – a circle which, instead of getting bogged down in an enclosed space, should move in an orbit which will allow each individual member to move around the other while remaining constant both within himself and in his relationship to the outside world?

Perpetual motion is a fact: children grow up, parents change and material and emotional situations are never permanent. An effort of communication would make it possible for relationships to be continually readjusted as part of the evolutionary process.

Mothers realise this straight away. The baby changes so much in a short time and a mother needs to adapt herself constantly to his ever-changing needs. The conscientious, loving mother, who provides tenderly for her baby in his earliest years, very soon becomes worse than a nanny. She takes charge of everything he does – she takes all important decisions even though she says she wants the child to be independent. How can he be, if she still sits him on her knee when he's twelve, or spreads his bread and butter for him when he's ten? Instead, she should be discreetly taking note of the budding breasts or the down sprouting on the chin.

Some mothers find it very difficult to accept their children's development over the years. They would like to turn the clock back, stop them growing up and enjoy for ever the very special loving relationship which exists between a mother and her tiny baby. They drag out the time when the child is dependent on them as long as they possibly can – they want to prevent him growing up, and don't want to have to be mother to this person who so little resembles the tiny baby that filled them with joy.

That wasn't so in my case: nothing could have fascinated me more than to watch a character forming, curiosity awakening and a mind and body growing. I found it much more interesting to see you grow up than remain a child.

I don't feel the least bit sad that you have grown up. I would even be rather relieved if you would accept the fact.

Anyway, if I forget for a moment that you're grown up, you're the first one to put me in my place: 'Listen, Mum, I'm not a baby any more . . .'

That's true, but if you're not babies any more, neither are we mothers of babies any more, and you find that very much harder to accept than we do. On this point you couldn't be more conservative. You'd do better to open your eyes and have a good look round – today's mothers are not the same as they used to be.

Modern mothers

I can't remember now which of my journalist friends told me the story of the 'real Mummy'.

Her ten-year-old daughter was asked to write an essay with the following title: 'Describe your mother at work.' The little girl brought her work proudly home to show her mother, who read: 'In the evening, Mummy is busy: she does the cooking and lays the table, then she peels the vegetables and prepares the soup. Daddy likes that very much, and so do I,' etc. . . .

Her mother was surprised, and said, 'You were asked to describe me at work, not at home. You know perfectly well that I go to the office every day – you've even been round the office with me. Why didn't you describe me writing an article on my typewriter?'

'Because our teacher wanted us to describe a "real Mummy".'

This little girl was ten at the time, the same age as you were.

You've changed a lot since then, and so have we. We haven't just grown older, we've grown up. There was no way we could have questioned our role as women without questioning our role as mothers.

For several years now people have talked about 'new' women, 'new' men, 'new' romanticism and the 'new' right. It's high time we added **new mothers** to this list of transformations.

In order to re-establish communication between our two generations, you should start by reviewing your false image of us. It may suit you, but it doesn't suit us. We're no longer like those 'real Mummies' in your early school books. You're not our **sole** reason for existing any more – if, indeed, you ever were. We're still tremendously concerned about you but we need to keep a large part of our life quite apart from motherhood. As you get older we should have been able to think a bit more about ourselves and a bit less about you, at least that's what we'd been hoping. Our urgent desire for freedom explains why we get annoyed when you are too demanding, or too dependent on us. We have thousands of exciting things we want to get on with in which you have no part.

The well-known division of women into two distinct groups – those who stay at home and those who go out to work – is of very little significance now that you're nearly grown up. All women are at one in their longing to be free, knowing that they have at least twenty years ahead of them to live as they please, whether as liberated women, or liberated mothers.

There's a time for everything in life. We want to spend the present time on ourselves, while you're still young and we're not yet old. We want to spend it with you, of course, but not on you.

Going back to work, becoming a student again, getting remarried, rediscovering the joys of friendship or the pleasures of a skill temporarily abandoned, finding the time to catch up on lost opportunities – the decade between forty and fifty is the time for mothers to have their second chance. This mustn't be wasted – later will really be too late, and there will only be room for regrets.

Women's energy and activity at this turning point in their lives is often astonishing. Working mothers can at last go off to their offices and involve themselves totally in their professional work without worrying about what is going on at home when they are not there. Personnel departments are well aware that absenteeism increases amongst middle-aged men, but the reverse is the case with middle-aged women.

Frances, a senior manager in an advertising agency, was talking enthusiastically about her freedom: 'At the age of forty-five I feel young for the first time in my life. I had my first daughter at twenty without really knowing what I was letting myself in for, and the second arrived two years later. I was divorced at thirty and, as my husband only gave me money from time to time when he felt like it, I had to slog away like hell to bring them up. Now that they've got jobs and boyfriends, I wish they'd leave me in peace. I absolutely refuse to ask their permission to go away for the weekend, and I can't stand the way they get in a huff when they phone me and find I'm not at home.

You can't imagine how possessive they are. And it's not as if I get anything in return. For instance, they'll let me know at the last possible moment that they can't come on holiday with me because they've been invited to join a group of friends. They would make a terrible fuss if I did the same sort of thing! They certainly let me know when, in their opinion, I've failed to come up to standard as a mother. They'd really like me to live like a nun, but I'm afraid I'm not going to oblige them. I'm determined to have my freedom!'

Mothers who stay at home sometimes undergo astonishing transformations too. Many of them with large families, far from being content to settle down quietly and become grannies, change radically. They open shops, immerse themselves in local politics, take up social responsibilities, bridge or Italian, and generally turn their lives upside down.

Look out, children! The new mothers have nothing in common with the Mummy who was your private property, who chose – or perhaps accepted – to give up work when you came bustling into her life. Having subjected herself to your needs and routine during the whole of your childhood, she's now more than ready to claim her freedom. You're losing a slave, along with the advantages and disadvantages that her freedom entails both now and in the future.

In the immediate future no doubt you will have to put up with a few burnt meals and some badly washed clothes. In the long run you'll be better off because you won't have a 'poor old Mum' hanging round your neck.

Portrait of a 'poor old Mum'

When I was young there were always lots of 'poor old Mums'. It was an expression generally used by grown-up children; sons used it with admiration, daughters with compassion and, almost always, with a strong determination never to get like that themselves. It was used to describe those heroic mothers who sacrificed their own future in order to fulfil their motherly duty. There were more of them amongst the less well off, but the privileged classes produced a strong contingent too. The term 'poor old Mum' didn't refer to her financial state, but to her lifestyle. You recognised her at once by the number of things she went without:

1. **Lack of sleep.** Not only did she often stay up late in order to finish all her household chores, but her children never let her sleep in at weekends or on holiday. The genuine 'poor old Mum' is the last to bed and the first to get up.
2. **Being deprived of food.** She certainly wasn't thin, far from it, but generally she wouldn't eat things like breast of chicken, the tenderest bit of the lamb leg, the freshest crusty bread, the lettuce heart, the ripest peach or the last chocolate in the box. These choice titbits tended to be left for the smallest or the greediest. I have never been quite sure how I felt about this sort of thing myself – let's just say that in thirty years of being a mother I've always eaten the drumsticks and never the breast of the one thousand, five hundred and sixty chickens that we must have eaten as a family. (This is assuming one chicken per week, probably the average for urban families.)
3. **Sexual inhibitions.** The 'poor old Mum' often had a lot of children, and she dreaded an unwanted pregnancy more than anything else, so she preferred to curb her desires rather than risk another baby.
4. **Delicate health.** Overwhelmed by her duty to her family and frustrated in her personal ambitions, she could only really find refuge through illness. Unable to stand up for herself, she found it easier to be ill, letting her body express the frustrations which she had never dared show to her family, or to herself for that matter. When everything got too much, she became really ill and was able to put aside her burden on doctor's orders.
5. **Neglect of her cultural development.** Because she felt all her time should be devoted to her children, she neglected to take up activities or hobbies solely for her

own pleasure. She would knit rather than read, go to the circus rather than the theatre, watch only children's programmes on the television, etc. Some women, who had been to university when they were young, found their minds deteriorating from lack of practice.

6. **Lack of independence.** The habit of existing only through other members of the family created in her a real emotional dependence. She just became a sounding board for other people's joys and cares. Because she lacked a real identity of her own, she risked becoming a heavy burden on those around her at times of misfortune, such as divorce, widowhood, financial worries, etc.

Deprived as they were of so much, 'poor old Mums' certainly were to be pitied. But above all, there was a danger that they might hamper their children's full development. It's only a short step from 'poor old Mum', via over-possessive mother, to the fearful mother-in-law who stifles her children's emotional fulfilment even when they're grown up – and it's a step she takes with a disarmingly clear conscience. Nothing can be too much to ask when you know you yourself have given your all!

Do children love their parents?

This danger hasn't completely disappeared as there will always be women who choose this sort of life; but their number is decreasing steadily, although they used to be in the majority in Europe, particularly in Latin countries. Less and less women feel they need to act as martyrs in order to be appreciated and loved by their families.

Sometimes, when you take me for granted, or don't show me enough affection, I wonder if I'm being done out of something by being so much the opposite of a 'poor old Mum'. Because you've always been told that you've been a great joy to me, that you were wanted children, that my life, far from being constricted by motherhood, has been greatly enriched by it, you have ended up thinking of yourselves as a gift from heaven. In other words, it's I who should be grateful to you. A benefactor shouldn't be expected to feel grateful to you for the pleasure he gives you.

Was Françoise Dolto right when she said that children don't love their parents? (See the quotation on page V.)

It may be true that these selfish little beasts love only themselves, and are only grateful for their parents' love because it lets them get what they want – it makes them feel secure and provides them with everything they need. If so, then we must **teach them to love us** and to show us affection, and this requires a subtle flow of propaganda.

The only way to combat their natural selfishness is to repeat sort of advertising jingles to them endlessly, such as: 'You must be nice to Mummy and Daddy', 'You've only got one Mummy and Daddy – you'd better be nice to us if you want us to look after you', 'When you grow up you must give me back some of the love I've given you so generously'. Otherwise they'll get used to being little tin gods and it won't occur to them to give anything in return, especially if we haven't laboured the point.

There's nothing new in this situation. Do you remember the fourth commandment? It comes just after the three main ones concerning God, and exhorts filial love: 'Honour thy father and thy mother, for the days are long in the land which the Lord thy God giveth thee.' In contrast, not one of them concerns itself with parental love. Could it be that children's feelings for their parents have forever posed problems, while our own have always flowed naturally?

Is that an over-pessimistic view? Not as much as it seems. No one believes any more in automatic emotions; so if children don't love us instinctively, they can discover us, appreciate us, feel warmth for what we are rather than for what we represent. It's much more satisfactory to think that, as they grow up, they don't love us because they have to but because they want to.

There is another possibility – that a child really doesn't want to have a warm, loving relationship with his parents. This point of view is certainly hard to take, but less painful, perhaps, if you accept the fact that the way you've treated him and the way he treats you bear no relation to one another. Our grandmothers' perpetual cry of: 'But what on earth have I done to deserve a child like this?' breaks one's heart because there's no reply.

In the confusion of my different theories on upbringing, I am certain of only one thing: **people don't get the children they deserve, they get the children they're given**. Perhaps I came to this conclusion because, having an optimistic nature, I needed to find a way of restoring my morale at times when I found my children really too ungrateful, or life too unfair.

Because you don't choose them, and because after twenty years' hard labour you only manage to change their basic characters the slightest little bit, **you have to make the best of them**. After all, we must remember that our parents made the best of us when we were twenty, and they weren't always too happy about it.

Yes, I know: we were less selfish, more sensitive, more respectful, harder working, less materialistic, more responsible, more interested in politics, more . . .

When people say that to me, I make them think back very carefully. Aren't they concealing the differences of opinion that they had with their demanding parents? Have they really forgotten their fiddles and the times when they weren't strictly truthful? Are they sure they didn't despise the mentality and lifestyle of grown-ups in those days?

Certainly family relationships were very different in the Fifties and Sixties, but more in the way we treated one another than in the way we felt. Were we nicer, or simply more polite? We did what we wanted surreptitiously in order to respect the rules of a society which was still very hypocritical.

Nowadays, people don't do things for show, they don't care so much what other people think. When you just can't get to first base with the wrinklies you don't pretend, you just give up the whole thing as a bad job.

It sounds almost insolent when you say things like: 'Leave it alone, don't bother about it, it's my problem.' When I hear you talk like that I always think of my father.

There was certainly no way we would have **spoken** to him like that, but surely the disagreements were basically the same?

Young people talk to us on a different level – they are completely relaxed and open. It's up to us to answer them in the same way.

In order to meet on level terms we must face the fact that our relationships with the young are not all that obvious – we don't owe them everything, and our main objective isn't that they should love us but that they should take responsibility for themselves. It's pleasant to spend time together if everyone wants to, but not in order to sulk or say unpleasant things. Is that all we get for what we give you? One or other is bearable, but not both at once!

Once you accept that relationships with your children should be flexible, you find it much easier to communicate with them, and to let them know your current opinion of them. If the relationship doesn't seem to be working satisfactorily, you can review it – and you can work together to look for solutions to crises. You can discuss the future rather than going over the past or getting stuck in the present.

Very calmly, in a most relaxed conversational tone, not stirring things up or risking a heart attack, or preaching, one can suggest, softly, softly . . . 'I've been thinking about this a lot, and I really believe it's time you grew up . . .'

IX

There Is A Limit To Patience

Boys and girls, fathers and mothers, all have the same kind of clothes, the same way of life. Everyone is chummy, and this is a brotherly society which levels out all the differences between sexes and generations. And parents no longer act as models.

Businessmen in tight jeans and middle-class housewives trying to look like dolly-girls deprive adolescents of their healthy rebellion against their parents. You only rebel if there's something to rebel against. Adolescents can only achieve adulthood by symbolically killing off their reactionary parents. By rejecting the unavoidable and beneficial 'succession of generations' and refusing to become middle-aged and then old, parents are abandoning their vital role, which is to hand on the torch of maturity and responsibility. They are no longer pushing young people into adulthood.

This severe judgement (in *L'Express* magazine, December 1983) by Professor Serge Lebovici, a university professor of psychiatry in Paris, is a clear expression of the classic opinion of psychiatrists who are always ready to treat us parents as scapegoats. Everything is always our fault. If our children refuse to become adults, **is it because we are taking our time to get old?**

I'm very sorry, but I don't agree.

First, his arguments are based on false assumptions. Nowadays, dynamic young managers and their wives – who aren't necessarily middle-class – no longer play at being adolescents and immature dolly girls. It's true that our parents wear jeans on holiday and tracksuits on Sundays but the young people themselves hardly ever wear them any more. Their fashions are exclusively theirs and don't tempt us at all. What modern father would want to look like a Mohican or have his hair in spikes like a punk? And what mother would want to have a green stripe in her hair, or walk about in rags made out of clothes hacked about with scissors or bought, still filthy, from a secondhand clothes stall?

If a girl sometimes looks presentable, it's because she has borrowed Mummy's clothes, not the other way around.

And then, saying that everything can be explained by the fact that parents have given up their roles as ogres seems to me a bit outdated. It fails to take into account the fundamental changes which are taking place in the families of our modern society. There are many more types of family today, and the roles of parents within these families have diversified. You've got the classic nuclear family, the one-parent family, second marriage, the family with two working parents, the family with a working mother and a father who has taken early retirement, etc. Authority is therefore no longer indivisible, but has become diffuse and shared.

The more I think about it the less convinced I am that it's vital for my children to 'kill' me in order to become adults. Just as well, incidentally, because they have now lost their main reason for wanting to bump me off!

In the repressive society of the nineteenth century and the early part of the twentieth, when the fundamentals of psychoanalytical theory were being worked out, it was vital to rebel in order to achieve independence, for obvious reasons: parents were there to prevent a full sex life, to repress desires and thwart pleasures. To young eyes, adults appeared to be obsessively against anything to do with sex.

In order to feel intellectually liberated, as well as instinctively and emotionally, there was only one thing to do, and that was to throw Mother and Father's prohibitions out of the window.

The sexual revolution inevitably had an effect on other aspects of daily life. Once battle had been joined with parents over this vital terrain – far be it from me to play down in any way the importance of sexuality – it was only logical to oppose them over other values they held dear. Even though it meant that they might come round to our values in the course of time.

This philosophy of confrontation was still entirely valid in the Fifties and Sixties. At that time your parents didn't always approve of you having an affair. In any case, not openly, under the parental roof. If you wanted to discover the joys of being together somewhere other than in the back of a car or in a rather sordid hotel bedroom, the only thing to do was to find a bolthole somewhere, even if it was without running water or central heating. Better an attic room on your own than a child's bedroom under observation!

Quite naturally, young people wanted to move out as soon as possible.

May, 1968, the time of the great student revolt, marked the peak moment for living in the unfurnished flat of old six-storey buildings where young 'revolutionaries' lived and loved in freedom.

An ideal status: the hermit crab

On the other hand, today's adolescents no longer need to move out in order to be able to make love. That is the big difference to which we haven't yet worked out the necessary reaction. Rather than looking back to the old-fashioned philosophy of nineteenth-century puritanical families, it's up to us to create a new family atmosphere.

This must be constructive rather than systematically antagonistic.

In fact, our children reject us less and less, because we don't stop them from doing what they like. Some of them may regret this new state of affairs, because the old system gave them more scope to assert their antagonism and to be aggressive as they grew up, but it's not worth trying to bring back obsolete restrictions just for their sake!

This leads us on to wondering whether or not our children remain cocooned in childhood simply because it's the most marvellous state to be in. If you really think about it, they have no worries about board and lodging, taxes or bills, and they no longer even have serious rows with Mummy and Daddy, the breadwinners – why on earth should they want to take on responsibility for themselves? They've got used to living in comfort all their childhood, and they don't want to give it up now.

In any case, whatever they earn for their first salary won't be nearly enough to keep them in the style to which they're accustomed thanks to Daddy's senior position – and increasingly often, Mummy's too.

They can use their salary as they choose – they can buy and run a car, take long or short holidays, and buy the latest trendy clothes. They can even put a little bit aside, in case one day they decide to marry and have a family. As long as their parents don't chuck them out, they would really be pretty stupid not to take advantage of being able to live like hermit crabs.

'John is incredible,' marvelled a friend, whose son was studying computer science. 'He tells me that he would like to live on his own but, before looking for a flat, he says I must promise to pay his rent, rates and insurance and the gas, electricity and telephone bills for at least two or three years. It doesn't occur to him that he could rough it a bit or go without anything. He will have finished his course in a year's time, and will be able to earn a good salary, but he's decided that he wants to travel round the world after working for a year or two. He doesn't seem to think that he should support himself. There's no question of pride, as there would have been when we were his age. It doesn't worry him in the least that we should have to pay for him.'

The way these post-adolescents get themselves enmeshed in our lives is the real problem. They sponge off us shamelessly, invading our territory just when we're finally hoping for some peace and quiet.

I am sure that there are many more parents who feel this way than there are couples who want to hang on to their grown-up babies.

In fact, these young people are much more likely to mess up our lives than we are to annoy them. They find they can really put up with us quite well as parents – don't forget, only six per cent leave home because of disagreements.

Therefore, it's up to us to take the initiative and to renegotiate the terms for our long-drawn-out life together.

Conditions for cohabitation

Parents are united in their opinion that patience has its limits, and they should therefore take the trouble to fix these limits.

It's necessary to be sure in your own mind first, and then pass on those views to the other interested parties.

Being in a position to say 'Well, I did warn you' seems to me the only way we can introduce a more or less consistent policy, by setting out in advance a framework encompassing both principles and financial arrangements. Then it is essential to stick to the general outlines of the programme whether or not the other family participants like it.

In order to set out the rules governing our relationships and the conditions for possible cohabitation, or its extension, I'm going to employ a four-stage system which I found in some fairly basic American-style manual on psychology. There's nothing particularly original about it, but it does help straighten out one's ideas with the minimum of subjectivity. After all, subjectivity is the most dominating factor when a mother starts thinking about her children!

1. Fix an absolute limit

Until what age can grown-up children reasonably expect to go on living at home? At what stage should they assume responsibility for themselves? How many times should you allow them to fail an exam? What are the criteria for calculating the cost of their independence? How many parking tickets should they be allowed each year when they use the car? What sort of financial scale should they be on – full living costs or just enough for pocket money? Up until what hour at night can their friends ring the door-bell or telephone them?

If you're not prepared to put up with a gang of friends invading the living room on Sunday after lunch, just when you want to settle down peacefully to listen to some classical music, **you must say so**. Not just a hint, vague indications or heavy sighs. Don't say it under your breath but speak out loud and clear. Even if it means your own child disappears every weekend the moment the last mouthful of Sunday lunch has been gulped down. (See point number 2 for the consequences.)

On the other hand, if you prefer to have them around your house, however inconvenient their invasion may be, you must admit it and not risk alienating them, being apparently welcoming but then making barbed comments so that no one is happy.

A divorced switchboard operator of forty-five, a union official who lives with her daughter of eighteen and her son of twenty-one, says: 'I am wonderfully happy with my pair, for I fit in completely with their way of life. Last year, for example, when my son was still in the army, he used to come home on leave once a fortnight with three friends. They slept anywhere, on mattresses in his bedroom, on the sofa in the living room. You should have seen the house: it was an absolute tip. They cleaned out the fridge and any drink they could find, in two days. My daughter and I spent Monday evenings clearing up their mess.'

'Do you find it reasonable, that they should turn your household upside down and leave without tidying up?'

'It's quite simple for me, you see: I've made a choice. Either I accept everything with good humour and live their way, or they will take off like all their friends, who finish up here because it's the only place where no one makes a fuss when they stub out their cigarettes in the coffee-cups . . . I don't mind the lack of peace and quiet, I prefer to be surrounded by these young people than to be on my own. Do you understand?'

Some people will admire her patience and others will criticise her weakness. That doesn't matter. The important point for her is that she has made a conscious decision and sticks to it.

This clarity is fundamental where money is concerned. Why spoil your generosity by grumbling crossly every time you get your purse out?

If you have already decided to pay and you know that you're going to cover some expense or other – if you would really rather give your child what he wants than instil in him a sense of the value of money, it's much better to admit it. It's a perfectly justifiable attitude. After all, what's the point of earning your living if your children can't benefit from it? **It's better to indulge them while you're still alive than to leave them your money – which will have lost a lot of its value by then anyway – when they themselves have practically reached old age!**

On the other hand, if the younger generation's extravagance threatens to rock the family budget, or if you genuinely believe that by keeping young people short of money they are more likely to apply themselves than if you are over-generous with them, you must have the courage of your convictions and do what you think is right with a clear conscience. It's a perfectly justifiable attitude. After all, what's the point of earning your living if your money is always being squandered by the children? **You don't owe your children help and support for ever.**

These are two totally opposite points of view, and each is as valid as the other. So nothing is black and white in matters of parental guidance? You could almost say that, but because this is a grey area it's vitally important to fix a limit – to say how far you're prepared to go as a supportive parent.

2. Consider the implications of your decisions

When you say NO to a child he doesn't like it. So he gets his own back by crying and screaming, breaking things and refusing his food. He behaves like a baby again, and generally makes life impossible for his parents in every way. That is, until one day when the child realises that refusing him something doesn't mean you don't love him any more. When he gets to that point he's no longer just a child. In some cases, unfortunately, that moment never arrives. We all know some men and women who behave like spoiled children all their lives. They can't bear to be denied anything, and have to take their revenge if they're crossed.

Big children's revenge is remarkably like that of small children, whose method of punishing us is by more or less ruining our lives: they lock their bedroom doors to show us we're not allowed to invade their territory, they disappear for days and weeks on end without leaving any address, and they deliberately refuse to join in family celebrations. They always use the same unpleasant methods: bad temper, absence and silence. They blackmail us by making us worry and they show us that they are more important to us than we are to them.

Frankly, if we aren't prepared to pay the price for refusing, we might just as well give in. We should never show weakness in front of our children, whether they're two or twenty.

But I am hardly the best person to accuse parents of being weak. I only have to think back to the story of my Renault 5 to remember how far I had to climb down!

I have never, ever, managed to refuse to lend MY car to any of my children. Unlike their father, who in this respect showed good sense by never letting them use HIS car, I have absolutely always ended up handing over the keys when asked for them.

A dozen times, after they'd had a bump or a breakdown or had failed to let me have the car back when I desperately needed it, I swore I would never under any circumstances let them lay hands on it again. Every time I broke my good resolutions – I just couldn't stand the gloom.

When I think back, I can find psychoanalytical reasons for this weakness. My own father encouraged me to pass my driving test when I was very young, so that I wouldn't have to rely on others for lifts. I was extremely grateful to him for demonstrating his confidence in me at a time when girls weren't automatically encouraged to start driving in the way that boys were. The car, therefore, represents to me an intellectual and emotional symbol of modern education and freedom. A refusal to lend my car would, I felt, place me firmly in the camp of selfish parents who ignore their children's need for mobility.

This neurosis turned out extremely expensive. My young drivers' accumulated bumps and scratches demolished my no-claim bonus and quadrupled my insurance premium. As far as I was concerned, the limit had been reached. The time had come for me to change my ways, so I sold my car and bought a season ticket.

On the whole, I prefer public transport to family rows.

3. Planning a strict campaign

When you decide to modify your approach to your children, the irritating thing is that nearly all the actions you have to take are negative ones.

No more . . . Definitely not . . . Refuse to (say yes, cover up, pay someone back, tidy up, clean, telephone, lend, give, put up with – the list is endless!) . . . Resist. Let them sort themselves out, learn from their own experience, live with their problems, etc. None of these decisions is particularly pleasant.

Above all, they require great strength of character because it's often more difficult to change one's style to being tough and resistant than to being generous and expansive. It's harder to be strict than to be easy-going.

Apart from a few particularly selfish individuals, parents' natural inclination is to be generous rather than hold back, and to help their children rather than leave them in the lurch. They would rather increase their comfort, not restrict it and, if anything, they prefer things to run smoothly rather than to be complicated by disagreements.

When our children go too far, the only way to make them understand that we've reached the limit of our patience is to alter our behaviour towards them, always in the direction of restraint.

From weaning till independence parents' lives consist

of one long process from everything to less, from YES to NO and from full guarantee to limited responsibility.

It's a pity, but it is so.

In order to be consistent, a plan of action mustn't take into account the person at whom it is directed. The initiative must come entirely from the instigator.

Here are a few examples which determine the borderline between action and enactment:

. . . You can give up buying wines and spirits if you're sick of seeing all the drinks in the house systematically vanishing every time you go away. *It's no good expecting that they'll leave the drinks cupboard alone just because you've asked them to.*

. . . You can refuse to pay for their holidays if they keep on failing their exams. *You can't force a student to work if he or she doesn't want to.*

. . . You can give up leaping to your feet when they burst in, starving, at nine o'clock when you're in the middle of watching your favourite programme. *It's no good insisting that they come home on time or ring to let you know they're going to be late.*

Some parents will just shrug their shoulders at these examples: their children still do as they're asked and have a respect for television sets and timekeeping. They give up their seats to old ladies and drink up their soup even if they don't like it. I'm quite sure these parents are sincere and are completely confident in their methods of upbringing. I should just like to say that they are exceptions, and should regard themselves as privileged beings. There is only one thing about them which amazes me: what are they doing here, on page 112 of this book which is dedicated to ordinary mortals and their problems with their children?

4. Tell those concerned about the timing of your campaign

Once you've defined the limits of your patience, contemplated possible repercussions and got ready for the fray, you must tell everyone what you have decided. You must be honest with your children, and warn them of all the disasters that may befall them once we have taken away the safety net.

Simply telling them won't be enough. You have to remember the fact that children have very selective hearing: they hear absolutely nothing unless it's of interest to them.

I myself have uttered so many useless threats and provoked so many misunderstandings – the messages I tried to get across weren't even half-heard, they fell on totally deaf ears – that in the end I resorted to writing notes as the best form of communication. They have the same advantages as they do when used in business:

. . . *The writer is forced to clarify his/her ideas and know exactly what he/she wishes to say.* It is easy to exclaim in a moment of exasperation 'I'm fed up with you . . . don't expect me to do any more for you . . . you only think about yourself . . . I never thought you could do such a thing . . .' It is entirely different when you put it down in black and white, after due consideration. Letters avoid those dramatic scenes which are always painful for those who suffer them and make those who start them look ridiculous.

. . . *It is impossible for the recipient to ignore them and claim that he/she wasn't warned.* Spoken words get forgotten, but written words are always there to be seen. Even when they are torn up they stick in the mind and pave the way for future decisions.

. . . *They are a convenient way of making a preliminary approach which can provide a basis for discussion.* Limits set by parents are not necessarily fair or logical; they may have let themselves get carried away by bad temper, or not have given due consideration to the circumstances. By writing down the terms of the proposed contract, you allow the other party to plead his cause, to put forward extra details or suggest counter-proposals. This is particularly true when establishing financial agreements, which are always more realistic when they are adjusted to take account of the claims and

> comments of those concerned. It is always better to make your first proposal appear somewhat on the mean side; like everybody else, young people are better at discovering that they need more than that you have been over-generous in your calculations.

As there are some people who have no gift for writing, I can also recommend the aural method: make a cassette recording. One father told me that he used this system for several years with his children, always with great success. He made good use of the time he spent travelling on business to confide to them his thoughts concerning their future. He feels that although he is often away he must have had a greater influence on his family than a father who is always at home but who doesn't dare voice his thoughts.

Finally, if you prefer more direct communication, a face-to-face interview in the style of 'Sit down, my boy/my dear, I have something important to say to you . . .' I must stress the need to plan the meeting carefully:

Vital. Arrange a rendezvous in advance, don't plunge into your little speech just as people are about to dash out of the house. A date fixed several days ahead will heighten the anxiety of the interviewee, and therefore make him more receptive.
Important. Avoid the early part of the day. They will still be half-asleep and won't take in anything. Be careful too about the evening, when you are liable to constant interruption by the telephone. It is often best to have lunch together, somewhere not too expensive, away from the rest of the family – a modest restaurant or bar, for it wouldn't look good to spend as much on this quiet meal as you intend to hand out as a weekly allowance.
Necessary. If it is a matter of long-term decisions – and, for young people, anything beyond the end of the month is long-term – don't ever think that saying once will be enough. Be prepared for several follow-up sessions.

I should add that, for this kind of discussion between you and your child, you should avoid having anyone else present; any important declaration made in front of a third party, particularly a brother or a sister, loses its importance and effectiveness.

All this ceremony may seem excessive; yet it can help parents go through with their decisions. It is never easy where everyday clashes are involved; but it becomes really difficult, even painful, when it comes to telling one of your children it's time he left home.

X

Time To Leave

Having exhausted all her arguments and all her patience, the mother of a girl who kept failing the first year of her course in psychology and sociology went to consult an eminent specialist:

Mother: I have come back to see you again about my daughter, who is twenty-two. Two years ago you advised me to send her abroad or to stay with relations in another part of the country so that she could become more independent, and get well away from her young brother and from me. I have tried sending her abroad, where she went as an au pair to a charming family, then to my parents in the country. After that I sent her to an aunt and finally to her father. Each time she came back sooner than planned, having given up all idea of getting a job or of studying.
For some time now she has been absolutely unbearable. She flies into a temper, breaks anything that comes to hand, throws things out of the window and has punch-ups with her brother.

Doctor: This is more worrying. Fits of temper at sixteen or seventeen are understandable but at twenty-two they are quite unacceptable, unless they hide a real pathological condition. We will give her a psychological assessment to see if there is something more serious.

Mother: She's already been assessed; there was nothing really out of the ordinary. She has had therapy. At least, she went about five or six times, then gave up. Her excuse was that the psychiatrist lived too far from us. I found another, just round the corner. She didn't like him. She said she couldn't get on with him . . . I just don't know what to do next, nor does her father.

Doctor: Deliver an ultimatum. Make it absolutely clear that this is her very last chance. She must understand fully that there won't be another, and that you will throw her out if she doesn't accept it or if she makes even the slightest objection. I repeat, OUT! And at that moment you mustn't go back on your word even if you are scared to death of what may happen to her.

Mother: It won't be the first time I've thrown her out or cut off her allowance. I've already tried twice. But when she comes back I always think that things are going to sort themselves out.

Doctor: You know perfectly well that's not true. Things don't sort themselves out just like that. Each time, she gets exactly what she wants: not to have to grow up, not to have to work, not to have to accept responsibility for herself. She's not ill, she doesn't really take drugs, just the odd sniff to scare you, she has boy friends, girl friends. So what's worrying you?

Mother: It's difficult not to think about all the things that could happen to her.

Doctor: Maybe, but if you want to give her a chance to stop all this before it's too late, you mustn't delay. Otherwise all that you are going through every day with her now may continue for the rest of your life. There is no reason for it to stop.

Mother: One thing is certain – for some time now she has become much harder. It doesn't bother her any more when I shout at her or tell her she's hopeless. What I say just doesn't get through to her any more. She finds more and more reasons to justify herself. Unemployment – 'There's no work for young people.' Her lack of skills – 'I'm not good at anything in particular.' Other people's stupidity – 'Employers are idiots, they don't know what they want.' She's got used to doing nothing, and now she takes it for granted.

Doctor: Why should she change? She's got herself into a position where she can exploit others, and it works. If the situation doesn't change she's never going to grow up. The only thing you can do for her is to make her accept responsibility for herself, whether she wants it or not. Do this for her, and stick to your guns.

It's unbelievable what parents will put up with, without complaining. And it's always the same. Young people exploit their parents' guilt to the utmost. I'm dealing with a girl now who is twenty-three and is having her seventh abortion. She would rather have abortions than accept responsibility for her own actions by taking the Pill every day. Her parents don't know what to do any more – they daren't let such an immature person run her own life.

So, if you're terrified at the idea of throwing your child out for good, go and see a psychiatrist yourself and talk to him about it. Make sure someone looks after you, but don't let your daughter see that you're afraid.

That's easier said than done, Doctor.

The mother who recounted this interview to me, almost word for word, was seeking your advice; aren't you one of the best known specialists in young people's drug addiction? Your statements have repeatedly attracted the attention of people concerned with the problems of modern youth, the pitfalls of today's society and parents' abdication of responsibility. Knowing of your sympathy and your compassion for young people in danger, she hoped you would give her some moderate advice, suggest some psychologically subtle way of guiding her daughter very gently towards independence. Instead of which, you firmly told her to throw the girl out, no matter what the risks or dangers!

When I last heard, she hadn't yet found the strength to do it . . .

This radical advice, coming from such a highly respected therapist, impressed me considerably. It demonstrated that a certain amount of firmness has now come back into favour, and it would certainly help you not to feel a monster when you finally decide one day that enough is enough.

Often, after exhausting all logical argument and all appeals to their feelings, parents realise that the only answer, when faced with an irresponsible and immature child, is to throw him out. To throw him into the maelstrom of life so that he will have to make up his mind to swim without Mummy or Daddy to save him. Even so, there is an ocean of parental guilt between acknowledging this and putting it into effect.

Pushing your frail child into the firing line can never be an easy decision when there is no one single event which justifies cutting him off in this way. All the young people who remain in this irresponsible state are frail by definition, otherwise their one and only aim would be to take up life's challenge.

There are certain incidents in family life which make this kind of break a bit easier: father loses his job, one of the parents becomes seriously ill, the parents get divorced, move house or find themselves in serious financial difficulties – any of these can provide an entirely valid reason for changes in status, habits or relationships. But, as we all know, problems never crop up at the right moment. Sometimes you have to have the courage to throw out a child with no other excuse than 'It's for your own good'.

Prince Charming lives ever after

At twenty-four, Virginia still had no plans for earning her living – she was quite content to live off her parents. She had already clocked up two or three abortions, and a few snorts of cocaine, and was completely disrupting her parents' life which, without her, would have been thoroughly pleasant. They got on well together, her father had a very good job and her mother had a career which she loved.

Nearly every evening, when Virginia had gone out with her gang of friends, savage rows would break out between the parents. The mother would shield her unbearable child, who was her only daughter and therefore her eternal baby. She never mentioned her own distress as a mother, but only spoke of the risks to her little girl. The father, on the other hand, let go his anger and indignation at having to support such an idle, useless child. He swore that his paternal love couldn't be expected to last indefinitely and that he was going to cut off all her allowances.

After the father had carried out his threat, the mother continued to subsidise a large part of her daughter's expenses out of her personal salary – a fact that she hid from her husband.

The mother's weakness was revealed when a tactless aunt let the cat out of the bag and, as a result, their marriage nearly broke up. Peace was only restored when the mother promised faithfully not to go on subsidising her daughter's idleness.

Six months later she told me, 'It's incredible! From the moment I stopped her hand-outs, and we showed a really united front, Virginia began to work. She lived from hand to mouth for a month and, as she's as bright as anyone else, she got a job as assistant to an estate agent. She's completely transformed – she's more fun, more healthy and much nicer to us. Her father has even said I can buy her a blouse or a pair of shoes from time to time.'

Virginia's case isn't unique. I could give several accounts, of boys as well as girls, who have pulled themselves together when there was really no other way out.

Yet it isn't simply chance that the two cases quoted in this chapter concern girls. Unconsciously, parents often have more of a tendency to keep girls at home and put up with the fact that they don't do anything. Boys have always been expected to go out to work as soon as they are grown up. Therefore parents think it perfectly logical to force them to get on with their lives by cutting off their support.

Because of our social and cultural traditions, the case with girls isn't so clear cut. Prince Charming lives ever after: a few years of feminism haven't been enough to kill him off. Prince Charming is supposed to solve the problem of what is to become of girls who haven't got jobs. He will come one day to take Cinderella away from Mother and Father, to offer her every comfort and a fuel-injected, tax-deductible carriage.

You must want work in order to find it

Every time they have to push a child out into the world, whether it's a boy or a girl, parents go through agonies before they are able to make the break. Each time, a few months or years later, they congratulate themselves at having been brave enough to take such an inhuman decision.

Once thrust out of the family home the exiles will often seek shelter with another member of the family. They try to take refuge with their grandparents, an older brother or sister, an aunt, or even a kind godmother.

I have been told about the case of a young man of thirty, who is more or less professionally unemployed. He is the immature father of a boy of two and for the last eighteen months he has unashamedly been squatting in his sister's flat, disrupting her life. She doesn't feel she can throw him out because of her baby nephew, although she is emotionally worn out and financially embarrassed by her brother's idleness.

Not all sisters are so kind-hearted, however, and not all grandmothers are prepared to turn their lives upside down in order to accommodate a grandchild. Generally, after staying a few weeks in this shelter, and having begged or borrowed several amounts of money the benefactor's goodwill begins to wear a bit thin. Therefore, for this big boy or big girl who's been banished from home there's only one solution: they must support themselves.

The most amazing thing is that generally, necessity being the mother of invention, they manage to do this pretty quickly. As an ex-drop-out said to me, two years after he had begun working in catering: 'In order to find work, it's no good just looking for it, you've got to want it.'

These break-ups don't necessarily always turn out well from the parents' point of view. Some sulky, unaffectionate children can never forgive the humiliation or the annoyance of being deliberately thrown out. They cut their links with the family and keep away from them, thinking mistakenly that 'out of sight' means 'out of mind'.

Many parents are not prepared to risk losing their children in this way. It was to encourage parents to stick to their convictions that the Americans founded 'Toughlove' in 1977, as a mutual aid movement for parents who were victims of their own children.

People who understand and help

Like Alcoholics Anonymous, Toughlove is the response to the fact that the only people who can really understand and help you when you are in the midst of a serious crisis are those who are currently experiencing the same difficulties, or have done so in the past.

Muriel Hees, who did a report on Toughlove in 1983 explains:

> Toughlove is a group whose aim is essentially to exonerate parents, to prevent them becoming the victims of children who are incapable of understanding the love their parents have for them, or of responding to it. When there is a crisis, it must be resolved and not just dodged . . .
>
> Alcohol and drugs are the main preoccupations of the parents who approach Toughlove. They are the problems of middle-class white Americans – at least you do not see poor people or Blacks here; not for their children the excuse of destitution or unemployment . .
>
> The philosophy of Toughlove is aimed at parents who are defeated, overwhelmed. It no longer matters why and how, it is a question of being realistic and putting an end to an intolerable situation, quickly and effectively. The Toughlove manual points out: 'It is not important to know why they behave like that, it is a matter of deciding whether you wish to live with someone who behaves in a destructive manner . .

Feeling guilty reduces your strength, and you need all your strength.'

As always with trans-Atlantic life styles, my first reaction when I heard of this association was to smile and say: 'The Americans are crazy!' On second thoughts, I had to agree that the very fact of meeting other parents in the same situation, of being able to express one's fears and realise that thousands of other couples are fighting the same battles, could be very helpful.

Anyway, is it so different when we confide family problems to our colleagues or friends? What else are we looking for when we seek the advice of a psychotherapist? A friendly listener – definitely outside the family – who can reassure us about our maternal attitude. I say 'maternal' deliberately, because fathers are less inclined to confide in other people; pride prevents them from complaining to a third party about children they're ashamed of.

Amongst my close friends, I know of three girls with anorexia, aged seventeen, twenty and twenty-three. They are all intelligent, friendly and pretty. The eldest is even married, and a medical student. All three lost so much weight that they had to go into hospital.

The three mothers are outgoing, active, each with more than one child. Two of them have lived with the girl's father for more than twenty years, and are typical well-balanced couples. The reason I am giving all these details is because there is a tendency to believe that such disasters only happen in families which have split up, and where there are 'bad' parents. These three women have suffered agonies watching their children killing themselves through lack of nourishment. Above all they have been upset to notice a sort of vague disapproval surrounding them. They all feel that the only people who understand them are those who have been through a similar sort of experience.

Indeed, it is only when they realise that what seems so terrible to them is really quite commonplace that parents can get their thoughts straight, and accept that their children are no worse than most – they can then relieve themselves of some of their guilt. In the kingdom of the blind there is no need to develop a complex because you can't see straight!

The only really useful bit of advice

It was during one of our family sessions of washing our dirty linen that I realised my relationships with you had been much too subjective and emotional. By asking you for things that you had no intention of giving me, and trying to give you things that you didn't want, I was in danger of making what was already a tense atmosphere very much worse. So I decided to listen to some excellent advice from the psychologist friend who was helping me to sort out my washing:

'The only person you can really expect to influence in any way at this stage, and whose behaviour you can alter, is YOU. Since you cannot change your children, present them with a different sort of mother.'

The day I accepted that I could no longer hope to teach you anything, that if you refuse categorically to understand certain things, then my going on and on would achieve nothing, that what I **said** passed unnoticed but that what I **did** still had an effect, that my bad temper was useless but that my good temper could still help to hold things together, is the day when I think I made a positive step in the direction of true wisdom!

In an area where each set of circumstances is unique, so that it is impossible to establish a general rule for improving complicated relationships, this is undoubtedly the only really useful bit of advice that I have ever been given: **Try and change yourself, don't exhaust yourself trying to change others.**

Further, this advice has the advantage that it can be applied to all circumstances, all conflicts, and all parents.

For the parents too, it is time to grow up!

Conclusion

Please Hurry Up And Grow Up A Bit!

I know, you have thousands of good reasons for behaving as you do. If you can't be bothered to make the effort to be civilised, if you disrupt my daily life, if you behave in an uncontrolled and messy way, if you damage everything around you – objects as well as feelings – you do it because you are young.

It is difficult to be young. I remember it very well.

I have always considered the notion of 'the best days of your life' fairly stupid. The 'best days' are the times when you feel relaxed, on good terms with yourself. You need to have been a grown-up for quite a long time to reach that stage, to achieve harmony within yourself.

Everyone envies you for being twenty years old, and yet nothing is more disturbing and complicated. Young people are admired; they are full of complexes. They are supposed to possess enthusiasm and vigour; they brood over problems and uncertainties. They are considered lighthearted; their doubts pile up at the threshold of adulthood. None of this will subside until much later, when they have got used to the routine of life.

As for love, you seek it, you believe in it, but as yet you scarcely know its joys, more probably its disappointments and unhappiness.

You make me really sad, with all your complexes, your doubts and sighs, your concealments and your bloody stupidity!

Here I go, starting to act the big-hearted mother once more. Here I go yet again, finding excuses for you.

Now that I have voiced my reproaches, my irritations,

my anxieties, my disappointments and my frustrations, I feel so much better. I have got rid of my anger, and I realise now that I have hardly any resentment left.

I have grown older while writing this book. I am less youthful in my maternal ways, but our relationship may well be better for that.

However, it takes two people to establish a sound relationship. Two to want it in the first place, two to work at it afterwards. Two to play the game of tenderness.

One thing is certain: as far as I'm concerned, I've given up battling on alone against your indifference. So I shall wait for you to take the initiative to retie the knot which has come loose.

Before we can find each other again, you will have to grow up a bit. You must find out – without my having to tell you – that genuine tenderness is a vital asset. It makes people want to give pleasure to someone else for no other reason than to give pleasure to that person. Not a childish tenderness, which always has a greater or lesser ulterior motive, but the true depth of adult warmth and caring.

Between a mother and her adult child this can be a most rewarding experience.

There still lie ahead of us perhaps twenty years in which we can benefit from this relationship. After that, I will be on the last lap. My hair will be too white and my heart too fragile for us to be able to treat each other as equals at that time. My frailty will upset the balance between us.

It's now, immediately, without delay, that I truly want to be friends with you.

Perhaps you won't feel such a need or desire. It happens more often than one might think, that adults 'forget' their parents. I know one dear old lady, kind-hearted and devoted, who sees her son approximately once a year. She can never understand why; nor, I dare say, can he.

You cannot choose your parents, just as you cannot choose your children. Since I want you to become adult and responsible, I must also accept the idea that you may choose to forget me.

In that case, I shall work hard not to let either of us feel too guilty.

Whatever the future may hold, you must understand that I shall always have wonderful memories of your childhood.

You too?